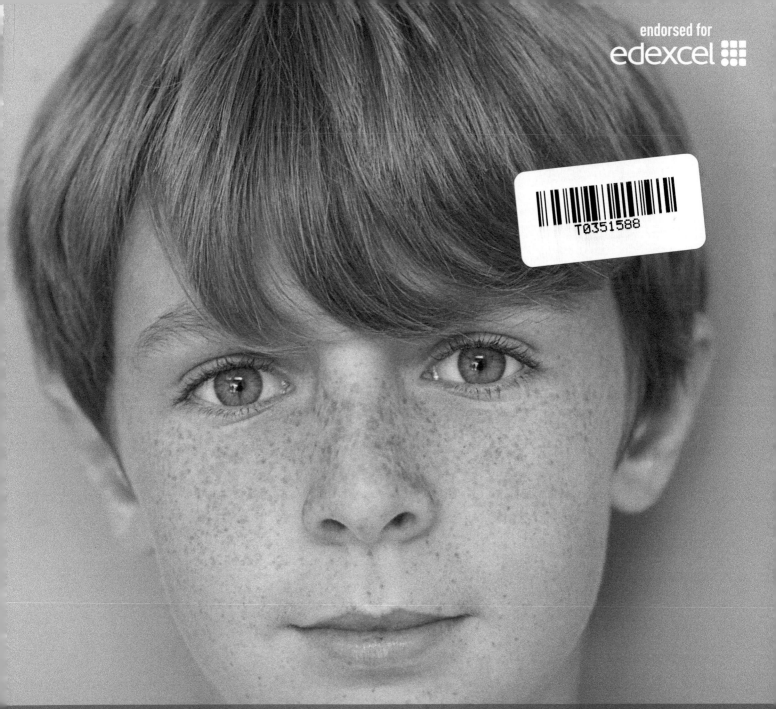

Edexcel GCSE (9-1)
Religious Studies B

Paper 1: Religion and Ethics: Christianity

Series Editor: Lynne Gibson   Author: Lynne Gibson

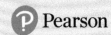

Pearson

Published by Pearson Education Limited, 80 Strand, London, WC2R 0RL.

www.pearsonschoolsandfecolleges.co.uk

Copies of official specifications for all Edexcel qualifications may be found on the website: www.edexcel.com

Text © Pearson Education Limited 2016
Series editor: Lynne Gibson
Typeset by Tek-Art
Produced by Hart Mcleod Ltd
Cover design by Malena Wilson-Max
Picture research by Caitlin Swain
Cover photo/illustration © Heide Bensen / Corbis

The right of Lynne Gibson to be identified as author of this work has been asserted by her in accordance with the Copyright, Designs and Patents Act 1988.

First published 2016

24
10 9 8

British Library Cataloguing in Publication Data
A catalogue record for this book is available from the British Library

ISBN 978 1 292 13932 6

Printed by CPI Group (UK) Ltd, Croydon CR0 4YY

Websites
Pearson Education Limited is not responsible for the content of any external internet sites. It is essential for tutors to preview each website before using it in class so as to ensure that the URL is still accurate, relevant and appropriate. We suggest that tutors bookmark useful websites and consider enabling students to access them through the school/college intranet.

A note from the publisher
In order to ensure that this resource offers high-quality support for the associated Pearson qualification, it has been through a review process by the awarding body. This process confirms that this resource fully covers the teaching and learning content of the specification or part of a specification at which it is aimed. It also confirms that it demonstrates an appropriate balance between the development of subject skills, knowledge and understanding, in addition to preparation for assessment.

Endorsement does not cover any guidance on assessment activities or processes (e.g. practice questions or advice on how to answer assessment questions), included in the resource nor does it prescribe any particular approach to the teaching or delivery of a related course.

While the publishers have made every attempt to ensure that advice on the qualification and its assessment is accurate, the official specification and associated assessment guidance materials are the only authoritative source of information and should always be referred to for definitive guidance.

Pearson examiners have not contributed to any sections in this resource relevant to examination papers for which they have responsibility.

Examiners will not use endorsed resources as a source of material for any assessment set by Pearson.

Endorsement of a resource does not mean that the resource is required to achieve this Pearson qualification, nor does it mean that it is the only suitable material available to support the qualification, and any resource lists produced by the awarding body shall include this and other appropriate resources.

Contents

How to use this book

What's covered?

This book covers Christianity: religion and ethics. This area of study makes up 50% of your GCSE course and will be examined in Paper 1.

This area of study focuses on the teachings, beliefs and practices of Christianity. You need to understand these aspects of the religion within British society today. This book also explains the different types of exam questions you will need to answer, and includes advice and example answers to help you improve.

Features

As well as a clear, detailed explanation of the key knowledge you will need, you will also find a number of features in the book:

Specialised terminology and Glossary

All the key words and terms are written in bold for easy reference. Explanations of what they all mean are given in the glossary at the back of the book.

Activities

Every few pages, you'll find a box containing some activities designed to help you check and embed knowledge and get you to really think about what you've studied. The activities start simple, but might get more challenging as you work through them.

Can you remember?

Throughout the chapter, these features ask you to recall facts from previous topics to reinforce your learning. These features encourage you to draw links between different beliefs and understand how they are incorporated into people's lives today. This will help you to remember the information and be able to access it again later. Revisit these as part of your revision, too.

> **Can you remember?**
>
> What are the teachings of the doctrines of original sin and the Fall?
>
> Why is the Atonement important to Christians?
>
> What is the Christian understanding of salvation?

Sources of authority

Throughout the topics you'll find quotations from sources of wisdom and authority such as the Qur'an and the Bible. They are highlighted in separate boxes so you can find them easily and use them as a revision tool.

> **Sources of authority**
>
> *For God so loved the world that he gave his one and only Son, that whoever believes in him shall not perish but have eternal life. For God did not send his Son into the world to condemn the world, but to save the world through him.*
> (John 3:16–17)

Extend your knowledge

At the end of each section, you'll find a box containing additional information that will help you gain a deeper understanding of the topic. This could be an alternative interpretation, a short biography of an important person or extra background information about an event. Information in these boxes is not essential to your exam success, but will provide you with valuable insights.

Exam-style questions and tips

This book also includes extra exam-style questions you can use to practise. These appear in the chapters and are accompanied by a tip to help you get started on an answer.

> **Exam-style question**
>
> Explain two beliefs that Christians hold about the afterlife.
>
> In your answer you must refer to a source of wisdom and authority. **(5 marks)**

> **Exam tip**
>
> Make sure you can support your ideas with references to sources of authority such as the Bible or the 39 Articles.

Summaries and Checkpoints

At the end of each topic, the main points are summarised in a series of bullet points – great for embedding the core knowledge, and handy for revision.

Checkpoints help you to check and reflect on your learning: The Strengthen section helps you to consolidate your knowledge and understanding, and check that you've grasped the basic ideas and concepts. The Challenge questions push you to go beyond just understanding the information, and into evaluation and analysis of what you've studied.

Recap

At the end of each chapter, you'll find the Recap section, designed to help you consolidate and reflect on the chapter as a whole. Each Recap spread includes a recall quiz, ideal for quickly checking your knowledge or for revision. They also include activities designed to help you summarise and analyse what you've learned, and also reflect on how each chapter links to other parts of the unit.

Recall quiz

Christian beliefs

1 When, where and how did Christianity begin and develop?
2 What are the three main Christian traditions?
3 Approximately, how many Christians are there in the world today?

The nature of God

4 What qualities do Christians believe are possessed by God?
5 Why is the Nicene Creed important to Christians?

Creation

6 What role does the Bible play in developing Christian beliefs about God?
7 Why might Christians have varying beliefs about the Creation story?

The Incarnation

8 What does the Doctrine of the Incarnation mean to Christians?

Extend

At the end of each chapter, there is an opportunity to read and work with a piece of text related to the chapter's learning. It might be an anecdote or description of an event, a personal viewpoint or an opportunity to look at more sacred texts. Tasks based on the passage will help you apply your knowledge to new contexts and bring together aspects of your learning from across the course.

Extend: Christian beliefs

The Parable of the Sheep and Goats

Jesus often taught his followers using parables, which are stories used to illustrate a religious or moral lesson. Stories such as these contain symbolism rich in meaning and are easily remembered. Jesus used the parable of 'The Sheep and the Goats' to show his followers what would happen at the Last Judgement.

Preparing for your exams

At the back of the book, you'll find a special section dedicated to explaining and exemplifying the new Edexcel GCSE RS exams. Each question type is explained through annotated sample answers at two levels, showing clearly how answers can be improved. There are also plenty of practice questions, with more tips to get you started.

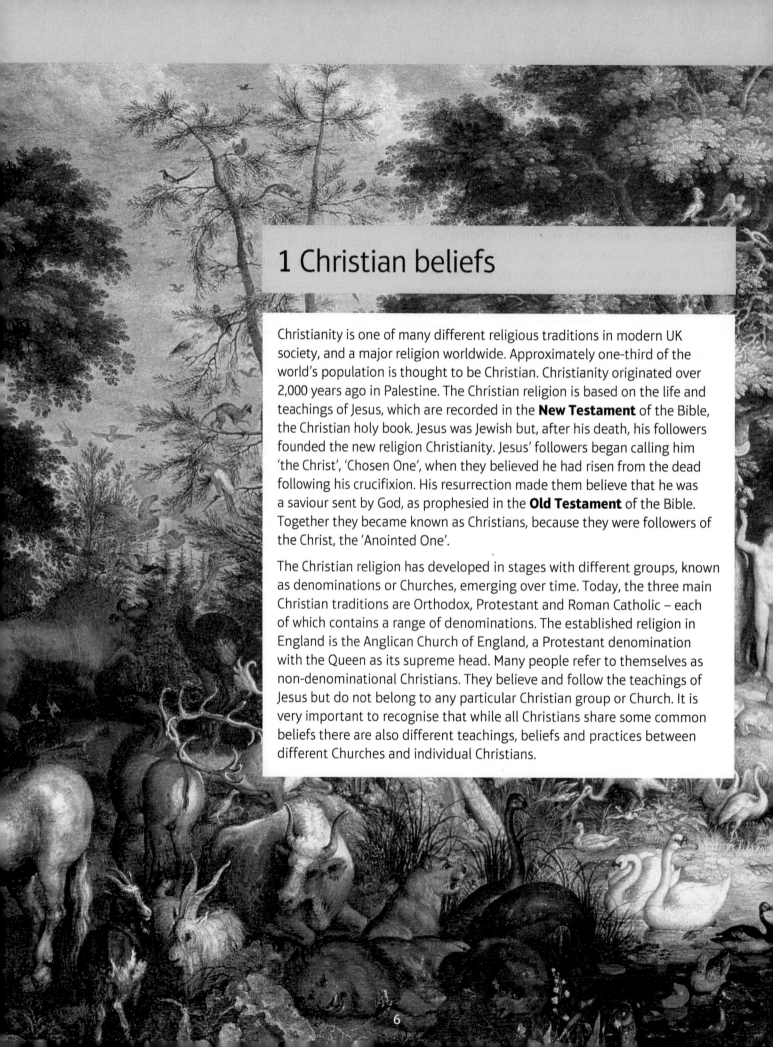

1 Christian beliefs

Christianity is one of many different religious traditions in modern UK society, and a major religion worldwide. Approximately one-third of the world's population is thought to be Christian. Christianity originated over 2,000 years ago in Palestine. The Christian religion is based on the life and teachings of Jesus, which are recorded in the **New Testament** of the Bible, the Christian holy book. Jesus was Jewish but, after his death, his followers founded the new religion Christianity. Jesus' followers began calling him 'the Christ', 'Chosen One', when they believed he had risen from the dead following his crucifixion. His resurrection made them believe that he was a saviour sent by God, as prophesied in the **Old Testament** of the Bible. Together they became known as Christians, because they were followers of the Christ, the 'Anointed One'.

The Christian religion has developed in stages with different groups, known as denominations or Churches, emerging over time. Today, the three main Christian traditions are Orthodox, Protestant and Roman Catholic – each of which contains a range of denominations. The established religion in England is the Anglican Church of England, a Protestant denomination with the Queen as its supreme head. Many people refer to themselves as non-denominational Christians. They believe and follow the teachings of Jesus but do not belong to any particular Christian group or Church. It is very important to recognise that while all Christians share some common beliefs there are also different teachings, beliefs and practices between different Churches and individual Christians.

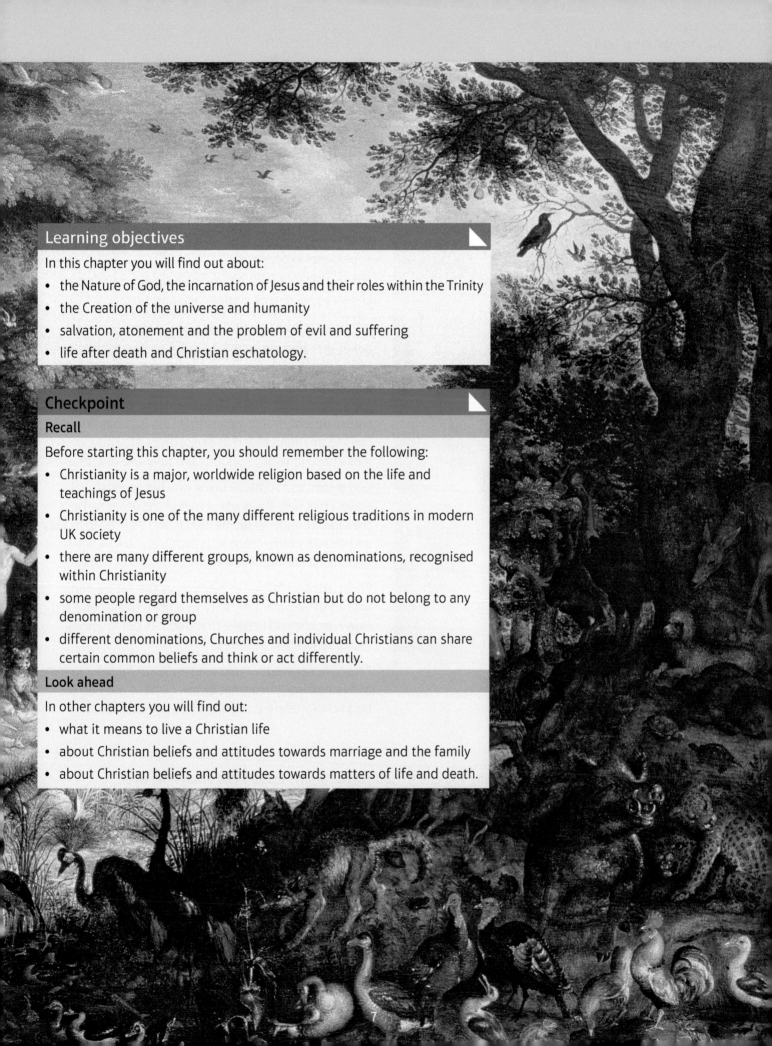

Learning objectives

In this chapter you will find out about:

- the Nature of God, the incarnation of Jesus and their roles within the Trinity
- the Creation of the universe and humanity
- salvation, atonement and the problem of evil and suffering
- life after death and Christian eschatology.

Checkpoint

Recall

Before starting this chapter, you should remember the following:

- Christianity is a major, worldwide religion based on the life and teachings of Jesus
- Christianity is one of the many different religious traditions in modern UK society
- there are many different groups, known as denominations, recognised within Christianity
- some people regard themselves as Christian but do not belong to any denomination or group
- different denominations, Churches and individual Christians can share certain common beliefs and think or act differently.

Look ahead

In other chapters you will find out:

- what it means to live a Christian life
- about Christian beliefs and attitudes towards marriage and the family
- about Christian beliefs and attitudes towards matters of life and death.

1.1 The nature of God

Figure 1.1 The Holy Trinity

Christian beliefs about God

Christians base their beliefs about God on:

- the Bible
- the official teachings of their Church
- the views of Christian leaders, writers and other Christians
- personal experience.

Things that influence a person's religious beliefs are known as sources of wisdom and authority.

Christianity is a **monotheistic** religion, which is the belief that there is only one God. A person who believes in one God is called a monotheist. The Oneness of God is important to the Christian understanding of God. Christianity, like other religions, teaches that God is **transcendent**, which means that God is above and beyond anything else that exists on Earth. This can make God difficult to understand fully and describe.

God is seen as a supreme being who has supernatural powers that defy the physical laws of the universe. He is therefore considered **divine**. God is also referred to as **holy** and **sacred**, which means he is extremely special, set apart from human beings and worthy of the utmost respect.

Christians accept that in many ways the nature and actions of God are a mystery to human beings on Earth. However, they do believe that God has the following characteristics or qualities.

Christians believe that God does not have a gender as male and female are human, not divine, qualities but God is traditionally referred to using masculine terms.

God is	This means
eternal	there is no beginning and end to God. He has always existed and always will exist.
infinite	all his qualities have no limits or boundaries in time or space.
omnibenevolent	he is all-loving and cares about human beings.
omnipotent	he has unlimited power and he controls everything that happens.
omniscient	he knows all things – past, present and future. It is impossible to hide anything from God.
omnipresent	God is always present and everywhere at all times. He is not limited by a physical body.
creator	he made the world and everything in it. God cares about his creation and has a plan for it.
pure and righteous	he is without fault and always does things that are right and morally good. There is no sin or evil within him.
the ultimate judge	God will hold each individual person to account for their thoughts, words and behaviour.

Some Christians believe this is wrong and that both feminine and masculine terms should be used to describe God.

The Trinity

One of the ways that most Christians explain the different characteristics and qualities of God is through a teaching known as the **Doctrine of the Trinity**. This is unique and fundamental to Christianity. It expresses the Christian belief that there is one God who has appeared to the world in three ways: Father, Son and Holy Spirit. However, this does not mean that Christians believe there are three gods. Christians believe that there are three equal but distinct persons within the Oneness of one God, which is called the Trinity. This helps to explain the different characteristics and qualities of God. In Matthew 3:13–17, the three individual parts of the Trinity come together in the act of Jesus' baptism. This idea is reflected in Christian worship today when Christians identify themselves with the Trinity in their own baptisms, which are done in the name of the Father, Son and Holy Spirit.

Sources of authority

As soon as Jesus was baptized, he went up out of the water. At that moment heaven was opened, and he saw the Spirit of God descending like a dove and alighting on him.

And a voice from heaven said, "This is my Son, whom I love; with him I am well pleased." (Matthew 3:16–17)

Christians agree that the way the Trinity works is one of the mysteries of the Christian faith. They believe that each part of the Trinity performs a special function:

- God as the Father created heaven and Earth
- God as the Son, Jesus, is the saviour of the world. He is believed to be the Messiah promised in Jewish scripture
- God as the Holy Spirit is an invisible spiritual power, which guides, helps and inspires human beings.

The Christian belief in the Trinity is set out in a statement or profession of faith called the **Nicene Creed**. The word 'creed' comes from the Latin word credo, which means 'I believe'. The early Christians had many different ideas about their religion and the identity of Jesus. There were lots of disagreements and

the Christian leaders thought it was important that everyone knew and agreed on the same basic beliefs on which Christianity is founded. So during the 4th century CE, they produced the Nicene Creed, stating the basic beliefs of every Christian. It was called this because its original adoption was at an important meeting called the Council of Nicaea. In some churches, the creed is recited during services as an affirmation of Christian belief in the Trinity. Another way that this belief is reflected is through prayer. The individual parts of the Trinity are supported by various sections of the Bible.

Some Christian denominations do not believe in the Trinity. For instance, the Unitarian and Jehovah's Witness denominations believe that Jesus and the Holy Spirit are inferior or subordinate to God. Meanwhile, the Church of Jesus Christ of Latter-day Saints, or Mormons, believe the three parts of the Trinity are one in will but independent in being. Most Christians, however, do believe in the Trinity and the Oneness of God.

Sources of authority

We believe in one God,
the Father, the Almighty,
maker of heaven and earth…
We believe in one Lord, Jesus Christ,
the only Son of God…
We believe in the Holy Spirit,
the Lord, the giver of life…
who with the Father and the Son is worshipped
and glorified.
(Nicene Creed)

Activities ?

1. Find and read the full text of the Nicene Creed, perhaps online or in a prayer book. Write out your own creed or statement of belief about the things you value and believe to be true about life and the world in which you live. Share what you have written with the person sitting next to you.
2. What do Christians believe to be true about God? Write your answer as a statement.
3. In groups, discuss three different roles that you play in each of your lives, noting the differences and similarities between them.

Exam-style question

Outline three Christian beliefs about God. **(3 marks)**

Exam tip

Always include a reference to the Oneness of God and the Trinity when explaining Christian beliefs about God.

Extend your knowledge

The **Apostles' Creed** is another Christian creed or statement of belief. It is called The Apostles' Creed because it summarises the teachings of the Apostles, a name given to the original twelve disciples of Jesus. The Apostles' Creed is regarded as an **ecumenical** symbol of faith. This means that it promotes unity between the different Christian churches. It represents the beliefs of most Christians. It is recited by Christians during daily prayer and worship. Use an online search engine to find and read the Apostles' Creed.

Summary

- Christian beliefs about God are based on sources of wisdom and authority like the Bible.
- Christians believe that God is the source of all goodness and will judge people according to how they live their lives. They believe that God is eternal, without limit (infinite), all-loving (omnibenevolent), all-powerful (omnipotent), all-knowing (omniscient) and always present (omnipresent). God is also the Creator of the world and everything in it.
- Christians believe that God relates to the world in three different ways: God as the Father who created the world; God as the Son, Jesus, who is the saviour of the world; God as the Holy Spirit, an invisible spiritual power that guides and inspires human beings.
- Most Christians believe in the Oneness of God and the Trinity. Some, like the Unitarian denomination, believe that God is a single entity.

Checkpoint

Strengthen

S1 Where do Christians get their beliefs about God from?

S2 What is the Doctrine of the Trinity?

S3 Why are the Nicene and Apostles' Creed important to Christians?

Challenge

C1 Why do you think there are different denominations or Churches within Christianity?

C2 What is the significance of the sources of wisdom and authority for Christian belief?

C3 Why might people disagree with Christian ideas or beliefs about God?

1.2 Creation

Christian beliefs about Creation

Creation and the Trinity

Christians believe that God, as Father, created the universe and that God in the form of the Trinity pre-existed the creation of the universe. They call this Creation. The first book of the Bible, Genesis, in the Old Testament, gives accounts of Creation and also makes a reference to the Holy Spirit.

Similarly, the New Testament in John 1:1 says that God was not alone during Creation but was with 'the Word'. Christians believe that 'the Word' is referring to Jesus, Son of God, which is discussed further in John 1:1–18. Jesus is, sometimes called 'the living Word' of God who became a man and lived as a human being on Earth.

The Creation Story

Genesis teaches that the universe and everything in it was created by God out of nothing. This took place, over a period of six days. According to Genesis, everything was created in the very beginning, precisely the way God wanted, according to God's plan. Human beings were created last, in 'God's image' and brought to life through 'the breath of God'. Christians understand this to mean that human beings have a soul: a non-physical, spiritual part of them that will live on after the body has died. They believe that this distinguishes them from animals, which do not have souls.

Christians believe they were given a special place in God's creation. God gave them the world to live in and they are responsible for looking after everything that God had created. This responsibility is known as **stewardship**. In ancient times a steward was someone who looked after something for someone else. Christians look after God's creation on behalf of God.

Sources of authority

Now the earth was formless and empty, darkness was over the surface of the deep, and the Spirit of God was hovering over the water. (Genesis 1:2)

In the beginning was the Word, and the Word was with God, and the Word was God. He was with God in the beginning. Through him all things were made; without him nothing was made that has been made. (John 1:1–3)

A summary of the Creation story
Day 1: God created light and separated it from the darkness. God named the light 'day' and the darkness 'night'.
Day 2: God created the sky. God used the sky to divide the water that covered the Earth into two halves.
Day 3: God gathered the water into one place, called the 'seas', and made land appear, called 'Earth'. God also created all of the plants and trees to grow on the Earth.
Day 4: God created the sun, moon and stars to light up the sky, govern night and day and mark the passing of time.
Day 5: God created all of the species of animals that live on Earth.
Day 6: God created the human beings and put them in charge of everything on the Earth that had been created.
Day 7: God rested, blessed the seventh day and made it holy. The universe was complete.

Can you remember?

- What characteristics and qualities do Christians believe that God has?
- What is the Doctrine of the Trinity?
- What is the significance of the Nicene Creed?

Activities

1 Role-play with a partner two Christians discussing their *different* beliefs about Creation.

2 Explain in your own words why a belief in Creation is important for Christians.

3 In groups, discuss what stewardship might mean for Christians today and how it might impact on their lives.

4 Research two Christian environmental charities, such as Operation Noah or Green Christian. Make notes on what they do and how they demonstrate a Christian belief in stewardship.

The Garden of Eden

According to the Bible there was a man called Adam and a woman called Eve. They lived in a beautiful paradise known as the Garden of Eden. God provided them with everything they needed but warned they must not eat the fruit of a particular tree. Their lives were perfect until they disobeyed the order, which led to God banishing them from the Garden of Eden forever. Christians call this **The Fall** because it represents a falling out with God, or rather losing his favour. It is also known as a fall from **grace**.

Figure 1.2 The Holy Trinity at the Creation

Christian attitudes towards the Creation story

Christians understand the Creation story in different ways, according to whether or not they have a literal or non-literal approach to the Bible text.

Some Christians believe that the Bible gives an accurate account of what actually happened – this is known as **creationism**. Christians who believe in creationism, or **creationists**, believe that the creation of the world and everything in it took place in six calendar days, exactly as it says in the book of Genesis. This comes from the view that the Bible is the inspired word of God, which is always correct.

Many Christians do not believe in creationism and think that the Creation story is not meant to be taken literally.

The Christian Creation story has been criticised by some scientists. This is because they believe in the **theory of evolution**, which is based on the idea that different species, including human beings, have evolved by changing their characteristics over time instead of being created exactly as they are today. They also say that science can prove that it took much longer than six days for the universe to be created. Many Christians share this view and believe that the word 'day' is a metaphor for a much longer period of time.

Christian beliefs about Creation have also been challenged by the **Big Bang Theory**. This scientific idea claims that everything was originally concentrated into an extremely tiny point that exploded in space billions of years ago and expanded into the universe. It is still expanding today. Many Christians say it supports their belief that God created the universe out of nothing and that, while the Bible does not contain strict historical or scientific truth, it is theologically true and reflects some historical and scientific truths.

The importance of Creation for Christians today

Christians believe that Creation is proof of God's eternal existence, ultimate power and his right to be worshipped. It also confirms that God is the source of all life and sets out God's purpose for human beings. This includes the responsibilities they have, such as stewardship. Christians believe that stewardship is a way of life – living in a way that recognises everything belongs to God. They commit their lives to God's service and are prepared to be held accountable for how they have used the abilities, resources and opportunities that God has given them. Christians believe that if they are good stewards God will reward them.

Exam-style question

Explain two different ways that Christians might understand the biblical account of Creation.
(4 marks)

Exam tip

Make sure you can explain why a belief in Creation is important for Christians.

Summary

- The Christian story of Creation is found in Genesis, the first book of the Bible, and describes how God created everything in the universe.
- Christians believe that human beings are different from animals by being given a special place in God's Creation and a duty of stewardship. The story of Creation reminds them of this responsibility.
- Christians have different views about whether the Creation story is completely true.
- A belief in Creation is important to Christians as it demonstrates that God is eternal, all-powerful and should be worshipped.

Checkpoint

Strengthen

S1 Where do Christians get their beliefs about Creation from?

S2 What happened during the event known as The Fall?

S3 What is the importance of Creation for Christians?

Extend

C1 Why do you think Christians have different beliefs about Creation?

C2 Why might people disagree with Christian beliefs about Creation?

C3 What can you learn about Christian beliefs from the idea of stewardship?

1.3 The Incarnation

Learning objectives

- To understand the nature of Jesus Christ as the incarnate Son of God.
- To understand the significance of the Doctrine of the Incarnation for Christians today.

Sources of authority

The Word became flesh and made his dwelling among us. We have seen his glory, the glory of the one and only Son, who came from the Father, full of grace and truth.
(John 1:14)

Sources of authority

Beyond all question, the mystery from which true godliness springs is great:
He appeared in the flesh,
was vindicated by the Spirit,
was seen by angels,
was preached among the nations,
was believed on in the world,
was taken up in glory.
(1 Timothy 3:16)

Jesus Christ

Jesus is the central figure in Christianity. The birth, life, death, resurrection and teachings of Jesus form the basis of the Christian religion and faith. Most of what Christians know about Jesus is found in the first four books of the New Testament in the Bible: Matthew, Mark, Luke and John, also known as the **Gospels**.

Most Christians believe that Jesus was the long awaited Messiah or Saviour of the world. They also believe that Jesus is the Son of God and the second 'person' of the Trinity. Another Christian teaching, mentioned in the previous topic, is that Jesus is the 'Word of God' who became human and lived on Earth. There is no explanation in the Bible about why Jesus is referred to as 'The Word'. Some people think it is because he, as the Son of God, showed the world the 'Word of God' through his teachings.

The belief in God taking human form as Jesus Christ is known as the **Incarnation**. The term 'incarnation' comes from a Latin word meaning 'the act of being made flesh'.

The religious term to describe the union of Jesus' humanity and divinity in the one person is called the **Hypostatic Union**. The Hypostatic Union is another mystery of the Christian faith.

Jesus as divine	Jesus as a man
Jesus is 'in very nature' God (Philippians 2:6).	Jesus was born as a baby to a human mother (Luke 2:7).
Jesus is omnipotent, all-powerful (Matthew 28:18) and omniscient, all-knowing (John 21:17).	Jesus had a human body (Luke 24:39), human mind (Luke 2:52) and a human soul (Matthew 26:38).
Jesus forgave sins, something only God can do (Mark 2:5–7). Jesus was without sin, only God is perfectly good (Matthew 4:1–10, Peter 2:22).	Jesus got tired (John 4:6), thirsty (John 19:28) and hungry (Matthew 4:2).
Jesus performed many miracles, too many to be all recorded (John 21:25). Even nature obeyed Jesus (Matthew 8:27).	Jesus expressed human emotions like amazement (Matthew 8:10) and sorrow (John 11:35).
Jesus was worshipped and prayed to (Matthew 2:11, 14:33, Acts 7:59).	Jesus worshipped and prayed to God (John 17).
Jesus was resurrected (Mark 16:1–20, Luke 24:1–53) and continues to be God (John 20:28).	Jesus died (Romans 5:8).

The importance of the Doctrine of the Incarnation for Christians today

A belief in the **Doctrine of the Incarnation** is important to Christians because it means that God, as Jesus, can understand what it means to be human. It also enables Christians to have, through Jesus, a personal relationship with God. Jesus is a source of revelation; his life and teachings reveal how people come to know God and what is expected of them by God.

Christians believe that the Incarnation shows God's immense love for human beings. In Jesus, they see a God who loves them so much that he was willing to take on human form and ultimately sacrifice his human life for them. His sacrifice is seen to balance the sins of human beings, and Christians believe that through following Jesus' teachings they will be offered eternal life.

Sources of authority

For God so loved the world that he gave his one and only Son, that whoever believes in him shall not perish but have eternal life.
(John 3:16)

Sources of authority

In the beginning was the Word, and the Word was with God, and the Word was God. He was with God in the beginning. Through him all things were made; without him nothing was made that has been made. In him was life, and that life was the light of all mankind. The light shines in the darkness, and the darkness has not overcome it.

There was a man sent from God whose name was John. He came as a witness to testify concerning that light, so that through him all might believe. He himself was not the light; he came only as a witness to the light.

The true light that gives light to everyone was coming into the world. He was in the world, and though the world was made through him, the world did not recognize him. He came to that which was his own, but his own did not receive him. Yet to all who did receive him, to those who believed in his name, he gave the right to become children of God—children born not of natural descent, nor of human decision or a husband's will, but born of God.

The Word became flesh and made his dwelling among us. We have seen his glory, the glory of the one and only Son, who came from the Father, full of grace and truth.

(John testified concerning him. He cried out, saying, "This is the one I spoke about when I said, 'He who comes after me has surpassed me because he was before me.'") Out of his fullness we have all received grace in place of grace already given. For the law was given through Moses; grace and truth came through Jesus Christ. No one has ever seen God, but the one and only Son, who is himself God and is in closest relationship with the Father, has made him known. (John 1:1–18)

Figure 1.3 The oldest known icon of Christ Pantocrator (Almighty or All-Powerful) – Saint Catherine's Monastery, Mount Sinai, Egypt

Activities ?

1. Identify three things you care about the most and write down how you demonstrate how important they are to you.

2. Design a webpage for an faith website explaining the Christian belief in the Doctrine of the Incarnation.

3. Summarise, in your own words, the differences that Christians would see between Jesus as God and as a human being.

4. 'Nothing is worth sacrificing your life for.' Do you agree? Give reasons for and against your answer.

Extend your knowledge

The Gospels

The word gospel comes from a Greek word meaning 'good news'. Some books in the New Testament are called the Gospels and they tell the story of Jesus' birth, life, death and resurrection as well as Jesus' teachings. It is difficult to say exactly when the four Gospels were written. However, it is generally accepted that they were written by Jesus' early followers, some of whom were believed to have known him personally. The Gospels are named after the people believed to have written them: Saint Matthew, Saint Mark, Saint Luke and Saint John.

Summary

- Christians believe that Jesus is the Son of God who came to Earth in human form. This belief is known as the Doctrine of the Incarnation.
- Jesus is the second member of the Trinity and is understood to be completely divine and completely human at the same time.
- Belief in the Incarnation is very important to Christians. They believe that Jesus' death, as a sacrifice for the sins of human beings, demonstrates how much God loves and cares about humanity.
- Christians see Jesus as a source of revelation, which helps them to understand what God is like and how God wants them to live.
- Christians also believe that they can have a personal relationship with God through Jesus.
- Christians base their beliefs about Jesus on the Gospels in the New Testament. These have recorded Jesus' birth, life, death, resurrection and his teachings.

Checkpoint

Strengthen

S1 What do Christians believe to be true about Jesus?

S2 What is the Doctrine of the Incarnation?

S3 Why is a belief in the Incarnation important for Christians?

Extend

C1 How might beliefs about the Incarnation influence the way a Christian lives their life?

C2 Why might some people find the Christian belief in the Incarnation difficult to accept?

C3 In what ways, other than through Jesus, might Christians think that God is revealed to them?

1.4 The last days of Jesus' life

Learning objectives

- To understand the important events of the last days of Jesus' life on Earth.
- To understand the significance of the last days of Jesus' life and his ascension into Heaven, and how they help Christians to understand the meaning and purpose of his time on Earth.

The Passion

Many Christians call the last few days of Jesus' life, particularly the suffering he endured, **The Passion (of Jesus Christ)**. The word 'passion' comes from a Latin word, which means 'suffering'.

In the Christian calendar, this period of Jesus' life is remembered during **Holy Week**, the week before **Easter**. The Passion of Jesus Christ and the events of Holy Week are recorded in the Gospels. The Gospel of Luke 22–24 contains accounts of the Last Supper, Jesus' betrayal, arrest, trial, crucifixion, resurrection and his ascension into Heaven. Christians believe that these events reveal the meaning and purpose of Jesus' life and help them to understand his role as a 'person' of the Trinity.

The Last Supper

The Last Supper is the final meal that Jesus had with his **disciples**, or close followers, on the evening before he was arrested. The Gospels say that during the meal he prepared his disciples for when he would no longer be with them in a physical sense. Jesus told them that he would soon be betrayed by one of his disciples and another would deny knowing him. However, he said that, after he had left the Earth, the Holy Spirit would come to them to help keep his teachings alive. Jesus gave his disciples two symbols, in the form of bread and wine, to remember him. The bread represented Jesus' body, which was to be sacrificed on behalf of all human beings, and the wine his blood.

Can you remember?

- Why are the Gospels important to an understanding of Jesus?
- What do Christians believe about the nature of Jesus?
- How does the Doctrine of the Incarnation relate to the Christian idea of the Trinity?

Figure 1.4 Leonardo da Vinci's mural painting of The Last Supper, based on the Gospel of John, is one of the world's most famous paintings

Figure 1.5 Jesus in the Garden of Gethsemane

Sources of authority

They left and found things just as Jesus had told them. So they prepared the Passover. When the hour came, Jesus and his apostles reclined at the table. And he said to them, 'I have eagerly desired to eat this Passover with you before I suffer. For I tell you, I will not eat it again until it finds fulfilment in the kingdom of God.'

After taking the cup, he gave thanks and said, 'Take this and divide it among you. For I tell you I will not drink again from the fruit of the vine until the kingdom of God comes.'

And he took bread, gave thanks and broke it, and gave it to them, saying, 'This is my body given for you; do this in remembrance of me.'

In the same way, after the supper he took the cup, saying, 'This cup is the new covenant in my blood, which is poured out for you. But the hand of him who is going to betray me is with mine on the table.' (Luke 22:13–21)

Today, the symbols of bread and wine are an important part of Christian worship in a ceremony known as the **Eucharist** or **Holy Communion**. This ceremony is known as a **sacrament**, which is an event or occasion during which a blessing is received from God. By taking part in the Eucharist, and receiving **consecrated**, meaning sacred, bread and wine (or grape juice), Christians remember the Last Supper, Jesus' death and the sacrifice he made for humankind. They believe the Eucharist is a sacred meal and it reminds them of the Christian belief that Jesus continues to be present in their lives.

Good Friday and Jesus' arrest, trial and crucifixion

After the Last Supper, Jesus is believed to have gone with his disciples to a garden called Gethsemane. He was arrested whilst praying there, after one of his disciples, Judas, told the authorities where to find him. The Gospels record that this was a time of great sorrow and torment for Jesus. Christians refer to the hours Jesus spent at Gethsemane as the 'agony in the garden'.

Sources of authority

Then one of the Twelve – the one called Judas Iscariot – went to the chief priests and asked, 'What are you willing to give me if I deliver him over to you?' So they counted out for him thirty pieces of silver. From then on Judas watched for an opportunity to hand him over. (Matthew 26:14–16)

After his arrest, Jesus was tried and found guilty of **blasphemy** by the **Sanhedrin**, the name given to the Jewish religious leaders and authorities. Blasphemy is seen to be a crime against God by either insulting God or pretending to be God. In ancient Jewish society, blasphemy was punishable by death. Pontius Pilate, the Roman **prefect**, a high official in charge of the city of Jerusalem, sentenced him to be whipped and

Exam-style question

Explain two reasons why taking a part in the Eucharist is important to Christians.

In your answer you must refer to a source of wisdom and authority. **(5 marks)**

Exam tip

Ensure you can describe the significance of the Eucharist, resurrection and ascension for Christians today.

crucified. For that reason Jesus was handed over to the Roman soldiers who mocked and beat him before leading him away to be crucified.

Christians commemorate Jesus' crucifixion and death on **Good Friday**, the Friday of Holy Week, and treat it as a day of mourning for Jesus' death. Christians believe that Jesus' death, ultimately, had good consequences for human beings. They believe that Jesus' suffering and death were part of God's plan, which can only be understood within the context of the **resurrection** of Jesus after his death.

The resurrection and its significance for Christians

The Gospels say that after Jesus had died, he rose from the dead three days later. This event is known as the resurrection. It is the central belief of Christianity and lies at the heart of the Christian faith.

The resurrection is important because Christians believe Jesus' ability to overcome death proved he was the Son of God and had a divine nature. It confirms their belief in the Trinity and an omnipotent God, who holds ultimate power over the universe he created, because only the Creator of life could resurrect life after death.

Sources of authority

… and who through the Spirit of holiness was appointed the Son of God in power by his resurrection from the dead: Jesus Christ our Lord. (Romans 1:4)

Activities ?

1 Consider the events in the last few days of Jesus' life. Discuss with a partner which event you think a Christian would find most important and why.

2 Explain what you think the following phrase, from John 14:6, means to Christians, giving reasons for your answer: 'I am the way the truth and the life. No one comes to the Father except through me.'

3 Look again at the Nicene Creed, mentioned earlier in the chapter, and the Apostles' Creed on page 35. How does each creed reflect the last few days of Jesus' life? List the relevant events mentioned in each creed.

Figure 1.6 The crucifixion of Jesus Christ.

Sources of authority

Jesus answered, 'I am the way and the truth and the life. No one comes to the Father except through me.'
(John 14:6)

After the Lord Jesus had spoken to them, he was taken up into heaven and he sat at the right hand of God.
(Mark 16:19)

Christians also think the resurrection shows that Jesus is their saviour. They believe he has the power to help those people who believe in him to overcome death. By forgiving their sins, Jesus can grant them the gift of eternal life with God.

The promise of the Holy Spirit

Christianity teaches that 40 days after his resurrection Jesus was taken up into heaven. This is known as the ascension of Jesus, and the Bible says that it was witnessed by his disciples.

The ascension marks the end of Jesus' time on Earth as a 'person' of the Trinity. Christians believe this means his mission, or reason for being on the Earth, was successful. He had completed everything God the Father had intended him to do and could return to heaven to prepare a place for his followers. Christians also think that Jesus' ascension prepared the way for the Holy Spirit to come to Earth, as Jesus had promised at the Last Supper.

Summary

- Christians believe that Jesus' suffering and death had a purpose. They also believe that the resurrection is the most important event in Christianity and proves that Jesus is the Son of God, the second member of the Trinity.

- Christianity teaches that Jesus was betrayed by one of his disciples, Judas Iscariot.

- The Last Supper is the final meal that Jesus shared with his disciples before he was arrested.

- During the Last Supper Jesus gave his disciples two symbols to remember him by. The symbols of bread and wine, which represent the sacrifice of Jesus' body and blood, form an important part of Christian worship today in a ceremony known as the Eucharist.

- According to the Gospels, Jesus also told his disciples that he would send the Holy Spirit, to comfort and guide them after he had left the Earth.

- Christians believe that Jesus was taken into heaven, 40 days after his resurrection, in an event known as the ascension. It marked the end of Jesus' time on Earth and the arrival of the Holy Spirit who would replace him.

Checkpoint

Strengthen

S1 What is the Passion of Jesus Christ?

S2 What do Christians believe happened to Jesus during his final few days on earth?

S3 What do Christians understand to be the purpose of Jesus' Earthly life?

Extend

C1 Why might some people say that the life of Jesus, as portrayed in the Bible, is not the type of life you would expect a saviour of the world to have?

C2 What reasons might non-Christians give to explain the resurrection?

C3 If you had to summarise the story of the Passion in one sentence, from a Christian perspective, what would you say it was about?

1.5 Atonement and salvation

Learning objectives

- To understand Christian teachings about atonement and salvation and their significance.
- To understand Christians beliefs about the role of Jesus Christ in atonement and salvation.

Sources of authority

For God so loved the world that he gave his one and only Son, that whoever believes in him shall not perish but have eternal life. For God did not send his Son into the world to condemn the world, but to save the world through him.
(John 3:16–17)

The doctrines of the Fall and original sin

Christianity teaches that all human beings are born imperfect and sinful and that this separates them from God. This teaching is the doctrine of original sin. The idea was introduced in the 4th century CE by St. Augustine. He taught that original sin came from the first human beings, Adam and Eve who disobeyed God in an event known as the Fall.

The **doctrine of the Fall** teaches that Adam and Eve were created perfect and lived in a world without fault. When they disobeyed God, they fell from that perfect state and separated themselves from God. Christians believe that the doctrines of the Fall and original sin

Figure 1.7 Adam and Eve's expulsion from paradise

explain how evil and suffering were first introduced and remain in the world today. They are important for understanding **atonement** and **salvation** because they explain how through disobedience and sin human beings became separated from God.

Atonement and redemption

The English word atonement comes from the idea of humankind being 'at one' or reconciled with God. Christians believe that this is necessary in order to be given eternal life with God, which is known as salvation.

Atonement is based on the belief that God, as an act of great love, sent Jesus the Son of God to Earth to be a divine sacrifice. Christians believe that Jesus' total obedience to God and his suffering and death were so powerful that it could offer **redemption**, the freedom from the consequences of sin, not only to himself but also the whole of humankind. This meant that the original relationship God had with human beings could be restored. Christians believe that human beings were unable to do this for themselves as they were sinners. Only the death of Jesus who was God, perfect and without sin, could achieve this by sacrificing his life, and in turn he extends salvation to everyone that believes in him, as depicted in John 3:10–21.

Within Christianity, there are different beliefs and theories about exactly how atonement leads to salvation. For example, many Christians agree with the **Moral Change Theory**. This is based on the idea that everything Jesus did, including his martyrdom and resurrection, set an example in order to guide human beings towards positive moral change, which would restore their relationship with God.

Another theory is that Jesus' death 'paid the price' or 'ransom' to release human beings from being enslaved to the devil, Satan, because of their sin. This is known as the Ransom Theory. Some Christians disagree with this idea as they say there is no scriptural basis for it. They also think that it gives too much importance and power to the devil.

An alternative explanation is the Penal Substitution Theory. It is based on the idea that Jesus' death 'paid the penalty' for human sin, which God's justice demanded. Jesus earned salvation by suffering punishment on behalf of all human beings. Many Christians believe that it is well supported by the Bible.

Salvation

In Christianity, salvation means being granted eternal life with God and Jesus Christ after death in a state of being known as **heaven**. To achieve salvation and be with God and Jesus after death Christians must be free from sin and the consequences of sin. The Bible suggests that there are a number of different ways that Christians can achieve salvation:

- being baptised
- repenting their sins
- accepting Jesus as their Lord and Saviour
- doing good works
- participating in church rituals such as the sacraments
- avoiding certain behaviours.

The vast majority of Christians agree that salvation is made possible by the death of Jesus on the cross. Christians believe in **justification by faith**. This means that salvation is available through the grace of God to everyone who believes in God and accepts Jesus as their saviour. However, Christian denominations have different beliefs about whether faith in Jesus alone is sufficient for salvation.

Generally, Protestant denominations such as the Church of England believe that faith in Jesus Christ alone is enough for a person to be saved, as long as their faith is deep and life changing and not just an intellectual belief. Some Christians believe that this kind of faith can be triggered through prayer in which a person **repents** of sins, asks for forgiveness from God and accepts Jesus Christ as the Son of God and Saviour of humankind. If Christians repent of their sins it means they are truly sorry for what they have done wrong.

Roman Catholics believe that salvation is achieved through faith and by participating in the sacraments, which are understood to be a channel for God's grace. The sacrament of baptism is seen to be particularly important. The Nicene Creed supports this by stating 'we acknowledge one baptism for the forgiveness of sins'.

Orthodox Christianity teaches that salvation is a more gradual process that happens within the context of living a Christian life. Individuals must try to become more and more like God. They believe that through the grace of God human beings participate together with God in the work of salvation. Orthodox Christians do not believe that there is any single 'salvation event'.

The significance of atonement and salvation for Christians today

The idea of atonement confirms the belief in a loving and all-powerful God who cares about human beings. Through Jesus, God made atonement possible, allowing Christians today to have a relationship with God. Christians also believe that atonement has made it feasible for all human beings

---

Sources of authority

Repent, then, and turn to God, so that your sins may be wiped out, that times of refreshing may come from the Lord. (Acts 3:19)

'Then Peter, filled with the Holy Spirit, said to them: "Rulers and elders of the people! If we are being called to account today for an act of kindness shown to a man who was lame and are being asked how he was healed, then know this, you and all the people of Israel: It is by the name of Jesus Christ of Nazareth, whom you crucified but whom God raised from the dead, that this man stands before you healed. Jesus is 'the stone you builders rejected, which has become the cornerstone.' Salvation is found in no one else, for there is no other name under heaven given to mankind by which we must be saved." (Acts 8–12)

His purpose was to create in himself one new humanity out of the two, thus making peace, and in one body to reconcile both of them to God through the cross, by which he put to death their hostility.
(Ephesians 2:15–16)

to be reconciled with each other. As a part of their stewardship responsibilities, they believe it is their duty to maintain this reconciliation.

The significance of salvation for Christians lies in their ability to be saved from the consequences of their sin. Most Christians understand salvation to be a spiritual rebirth or renewal that takes place by the grace of God through the actions of the Holy Spirit, as a single event or over a longer period of time. Each member of the Trinity has an important role to play in salvation:

- God the Father sent the Son to die for the sins of human beings
- God the Son sacrificed himself for the sins of human beings
- God the Holy Spirit works within human beings to enable them to understand the truth about God.

Christians can therefore only be saved by the Trinity as a whole. The term 'born again' is used by some Christians to describe the process by which they come to have a faith in Jesus and are therefore saved. Others use the term to describe the moment when everything they know or have been taught about Christianity becomes real for them on a personal level.

Christians all try to live their lives in the way they believe God wants them to and through following Jesus' teachings. However, many may argue that they do this as a consequence of their faith and not because they believe it is a condition of salvation.

Activities ?

1 Discuss with a partner what you think about the idea of always being able to make up for the things you have done wrong.
2 Draw a diagram showing how each member of the Trinity works together to achieve salvation for human beings.
3 Write a statement to explain, using your own words, how the Christian ideas of atonement and salvation are connected.
4 What do you think about the concept of someone else 'paying the price' or 'making up' for something you have done wrong? Put forward a Christian response as well as your own.

Sources of authority

Jesus replied, 'Very truly I tell you, no one can see the kingdom of God unless they are born again.'
(John 3:3)

Exam-style question

Explain the significance of atonement and salvation to Christians today. In your answer you must refer to a source of wisdom and authority. **(5 marks)**

Exam tip

Ensure that you understand Christian beliefs about atonement and salvation and can explain the importance of them for Christians today.

Checkpoint

Strengthen

S1 What do Christians understand by the term 'atonement'?
S2 Why might salvation be important to a Christian?
S3 What role does the Trinity play in atonement and salvation?

Extend

C1 What is an atonement theory?
C2 How do Christians believe they can achieve salvation?
C3 Why might some Christians refer to themselves as 'born again'?

Summary

- Christians believe that Jesus suffered and died on the cross to save human beings from their sins. This is called atonement.
- There are different views about how atonement works and there are a number of theories that try to explain it.
- Salvation is the idea that only a soul that is free from sin can be with God in Heaven after death. Christians believe that the opportunity of salvation is available to everyone through faith in Jesus, providing they are truly sorry for what they have done, repentant of their sins and ask for forgiveness.

1.6 Eschatology: Life after death

Learning objective

- To understand Christian eschatological beliefs, particularly as they relate to life after death.

Eschatology

In Christianity, **eschatology** is the study of what happens at the '**end times**' or the 'end of the world'. This includes death, judgement, the destination of the soul and the overall destiny of humankind.

The Soul

Christians believe that each life has a purpose and that death is not the end of our existence. They believe the resurrection of Jesus proved there is life after death. Christians believe the soul of a human being is **immortal and everlasting** and has an ongoing consciousness. It leaves the physical body at death and continues to exist in the afterlife – either in heaven, **hell** or **purgatory**. Souls that have achieved salvation and been saved from the consequences of their sins will either go to heaven or purgatory, whereas, souls that have not achieved salvation will endure their sins. They will be judged by God and sentenced to spend eternity in hell.

Christian beliefs about the soul have developed over time and have been shaped by a variety of ideas, particularly those of Greek philosophers such as Aristotle and Plato. One Christian thinker who has been a major influence on Christian beliefs about the soul is Thomas Aquinas (1225–1274). In his work *The Summa Theologica*, Aquinas taught that the soul is a conscious entity that can understand, reason and choose its own actions but cannot be destroyed.

Judgement

Christian teachings about Judgement, the **Last Judgement**, Heaven and Hell are based on the Bible. Christians believe that, because God is perfectly good and morally pure, human beings are accountable to God for how they behave. They also believe that God is perfectly loving, without evil and omniscient. As a result, they can trust God to judge human beings fairly. Christians believe that the judgement of God will decide the destination of the soul after death and at the end of the world or 'end times'.

Christianity teaches that Jesus Christ, the Son, shares in the work of judgement with God, the Father.

According to the Bible, Jesus will judge everyone who has ever lived and offer them the opportunity of salvation. Those who refuse will face another judgement at the Last Judgement.

The Last Judgement

Christians believe that the Last Judgement is where God will determine the final destiny of everyone, alive or dead, at the point of 'end times'. According to the Bible, Jesus will return to Earth at the time of the Last Judgement in an event known as the second coming or **Parousia**. Christianity teaches that the Last Judgement will bring about a physical resurrection of the dead. Traditionally, this is why Christians have been buried instead of cremated when they die. Some Christians do choose to be cremated after death because they believe they will be raised as a spiritual body, rather than a physical body, at the Last Judgement. They base this belief on an idea in the Bible that their physical body separates them from God and that after death they will be 'clothed' in a new body.

Heaven

Traditionally, Christians have understood heaven to be a transcendent, spiritual realm rather than a physical place in the universe. The Bible teaches that there is no sin, sadness, pain or suffering in heaven. Christians understand this to mean that heaven is a holy, happy and peaceful state of being with God and Jesus after death. Christian art often shows pictures of heaven but Christians agree that it is very difficult to describe accurately what it is like since it is beyond all human experience.

Hell

Christianity teaches that hell is a place or state of being where unrepentant sinners go after death. An unrepentant sinner is someone who does not regret the things they have done wrong and refuses God's offer

Figure 1.8 The Last Judgement by John Martin

of forgiveness and salvation through Jesus. A well-known image of hell, as an underground place of eternal fire and suffering, is based on the literal interpretation of biblical ideas. However, many Christians today believe that hell is characterised by not being in the presence of God after death. They think that the soul will long to be reunited with God, its creator. Therefore, the punishment and misery of hell is seen to be spiritual desolation or isolation of the soul. Some Christians reject the idea of hell altogether as they believe it is inconsistent with an omnibenevolent God and the messages of forgiveness and love taught by Jesus.

Purgatory

The Orthodox and Roman Catholic Churches teach that there is also a state after physical death, and prior to heaven or hell, known as Purgatory. This is a place where souls are purified and made holy enough to enter heaven. Christians who believe in this idea think that the time a soul spends in Purgatory can be shortened by the prayers of those still alive. Other denominations, such as Anglicans, reject the idea of Purgatory, although they do believe that the soul continues to develop and grow in holiness after death. The '39 Articles of Religion', a source of authority for Anglican beliefs, maintains that there is no foundation in the Bible for the existence of Purgatory (XXII of Purgatory).

Similarities and differences between Christianity and Islam

Beliefs about the afterlife are important to both Muslims and Christians. They both:

- view life as a test in terms of determining their afterlife hold beliefs in a place of eternal reward and a place of eternal punishment, alongside the idea of a Day of Judgement

Sources of authority

For we know that if the earthly tent we live in is destroyed, we have a building from God, an eternal house in heaven, not built by human hands. Meanwhile we groan, longing to be clothed instead with our heavenly dwelling, because when we are clothed, we will not be found naked. For while we are in this tent, we groan and are burdened, because we do not wish to be unclothed but to be clothed instead with our heavenly dwelling, so that what is mortal may be swallowed up by life. Now the one who has fashioned us for this very purpose is God, who has given us the Spirit as a deposit, guaranteeing what is to come.

Therefore we are always confident and know that as long as we are at home in the body we are away from the Lord. For we live by faith, not by sight. We are confident, I say, and would prefer to be away from the body and at home with the Lord. So we make it our goal to please him, whether we are at home in the body or away from it. For we must all appear before the judgment seat of Christ, so that each of us may receive what is due to us for the things done while in the body, whether good or bad.

(2 Corinthians 5:1-10)

Can you remember?

- What are the teachings of the doctrines of original sin and the Fall?
- Why is atonement important to Christians?
- What is the Christian understanding of salvation?

- share ideas in regards to resurrection.

Differences include how:

- Christians accept the sacrifice of Jesus to atone for the sins of the world whereas Muslims believe only the sinner themselves can ask for forgiveness
- some Christians accept the idea of purgatory, alongside heaven and hell, which is not seen in Islam
- Muslims accept ideas of angels who record the deeds of a person whereas Christians do not identify them with this act.

Activities ?

1 Explain to a partner what Christians believe about the soul.

2 Draw pictures or design a range of symbols to show what Christians believe heaven, hell and Purgatory are like.

3 In groups, look closely at the image of the Last Judgement by John Martin. Explain how the different features of the painting represent Christian eschatological beliefs.

Exam tip

Make sure you can support your ideas with references to sources of authority such as the Bible or the 39 Articles of Religion.

Exam-style question

Explain two beliefs that Christians hold about the afterlife.

In your answer you must refer to a source of wisdom and authority. **(5 marks)**

Summary

- Christians believe that life continues after death in either heaven, hell or Purgatory. This is because they think human beings have a soul that lives on after the physical death of the body.
- Some denominations also believe in an intermediate state before known as Purgatory.
- Christians believe that human beings have the opportunity to be with God when they die, depending on God's judgement and whether they have accepted salvation through Jesus Christ.
- Christians also believe in the Last Judgement, which will take place when Jesus returns to. The Last Judgement is when God makes a final judgement on everyone, alive or dead.

Checkpoint

Strengthen

S1 What are the Christian eschatological beliefs concerning the destiny of the soul and humankind?

S2 What are the key differences between heaven and hell from a Christian perspective?

S3 Which denominations believe in Purgatory?

Extend

C1 Why do Christians believe that God will be a fair and reliable judge of moral behaviour?

C2 Why do you think most Christians today think of heaven as a state of being rather than a physical place?

C3 Why might some people think that the idea of hell is inconsistent with an omnibenevolent God?

1.7 Evil and suffering

Learning objectives

- To understand the challenge Christians face in reconciling a belief in God in a world where there is evil and suffering.
- To understand Christian beliefs about evil and suffering.

Evil and suffering in the world

One of the biggest challenges to a belief in God is the presence of evil and suffering in the world. It can make people question their faith and the existence of God. They argue that if God is omnibenevolent, omnipotent, omniscient and omnipresent, as Christians believe, why is there so much pain and horror in the world? Consequently, some people draw the following conclusions.

- God does not exist because he would not allow human beings to do evil things.
- God does not exist because he would not allow human beings to suffer.
- If God does exist then his qualities and powers must be limited in some way, or he would do more, and therefore he cannot be all-powerful after all.

Others argue that suffering is part of what it means to be human, and those times of difficulty would otherwise be unbearable without God's comfort and support. Some people also think that in order to identify good we need to experience evil, and that we need to have sorrow and suffering so we can recognise happiness.

People's ideas and beliefs about evil and suffering can change depending on their experiences. For people who believe in God, **theists**, personal suffering can sometimes be a test of their faith. It can sometimes make people lose their faith in God or, alternatively, it can strengthen their faith. There are some people, **atheists** and **agnostics**, who either do not believe in God or are unsure about whether or not God exists, who have discovered faith while experiencing or witnessing suffering.

Figure 1.9 A pleasure boat rests on top of a building amid a sea of debris in Otsuchi town, following the tsunami on 11 March 2014, in Japan

27

Sources of authority

Then Satan entered Judas, called Iscariot, one of the Twelve.
(Luke 22:3)

The God of peace will soon crush Satan under your feet.
The grace of our Lord Jesus be with you. (Romans 16:20)

And I saw an angel coming down out of heaven, having the key to the Abyss and holding in his hand a great chain. He seized the dragon, that ancient serpent, who is the devil, or Satan, and bound him for a thousand years. He threw him into the Abyss, and locked and sealed it over him, to keep him from deceiving the nations anymore until the thousand years were ended. After that, he must be set free for a short time. (Revelation 20:1–3)

Figure 1.10 The Devil. Detail from a 16th century fresco

Natural evil

The definition of **evil** is 'morally wrong, bad, wicked'. Evil can also be understood as something that causes people to suffer. There are many different reasons for people's suffering. When it is caused by a natural disaster, such as an avalanche, earthquake, tsunami or disease, it is known as natural evil. This is because it seems to occur as a result of nature rather than human action.

Moral evil

Suffering can also come from the deliberate actions of human beings. Acts of aggression and violence, such as murder and terrorism, are considered moral evils. This type of suffering is known as moral evil because it happens as a consequence of human choices and actions. The word '**moral**' means 'right and wrong behaviour'.

Not all types of suffering fit clearly into the two categories of natural or moral evil. Human beings may cause suffering to others accidentally. Natural disasters and diseases can also happen because of human interaction with nature, including the misuse or abuse of natural resources.

The Christian response to evil and suffering

Christians believe that God is righteous and morally pure and that he will fairly judge and punish those who do wrong. They believe he can only do things that are right and hates wickedness. Because of this, it makes sense that God could not have created evil.

Parts of the Bible are honest and direct about the existence of evil and suffering in the world. For example, Psalm 119 brings the ideas of life's harsh realities and the grace of God together in a reaffirming and educating piece of Scripture that looks to God for help and support. However, the questions 'Where does evil come from?' and 'Why is there evil and suffering in the world?' have always challenged Christian beliefs about God. The existence of evil is difficult to explain and seems inconsistent with a belief in a righteous God.

The Devil

Some Christians believe there is evil in the world due to the existence of the Devil, also known as Satan. According to early Christian teaching, the Devil is an angel who was cast out of heaven because he rebelled against God. The Devil is seen as the enemy of God; he tries to turn people away from God and goodness, encouraging human beings to commit evil acts instead. In the story of the Fall, people believe it was the devil who tempted Adam and Eve into disobeying God. This act of defiance against God is believed to have brought evil into the world.

Satan is also said to have been responsible for the betrayal by one of Jesus' disciples, Judas Iscariot, shortly before Jesus was crucified.

Christians believe that the Holy Spirit can help people to fight against and overcome the Devil. Most Christian eschatological beliefs say that Jesus will overcome Satan once and for all during the 'end times'.

Others state:

That Satan will be imprisoned for a thousand years before eventually being destroyed.

Some Christians do not believe that the Devil or Satan is real. They think that the idea of the Devil is symbolic and represents human sinfulness, temptation and anything that goes against God.

Irenaean theodicy

Another idea put forward to explain the existence of evil and suffering is the **Irenaean theodicy**. A theodicy is a defence of God against the existence of evil. Irenaeus was a Christian bishop and philosopher who lived in the second century. He is known as one of the Fathers of the Christian Church as his ideas helped to develop Christianity.

Irenaeus taught that the purpose of the world was to develop the **morality** of human beings. Even though human beings were created in the 'image of God', he believed they still needed to grow into the perfect 'likeness of God'. Irenaeus said that God gave humans free will so that they could choose between good and evil, and therefore have a genuine opportunity to do the wrong thing. The existence of evil is necessary, as only by choosing to do the right thing could people achieve moral perfection.

Irenaeus believed that suffering and evil would help human beings grow closer to God.

He believed that eventually suffering and evil would be overcome.

The 'Vale of Soul Making' theodicy

John Hick (1922–2012), a modern Christian philosopher, built on the work of Irenaeus and developed a 'soul-making' theodicy. Like Irenaeus, Hick believed that God purposefully allows evil into the world and left people incomplete so they could develop their souls themselves, by overcoming evil and suffering. Although he accepted that God has some responsibility for the presence of evil and suffering in the world, this idea does not need to contradict with the perfectly good and loving nature of God.

Hick argued that God had to give human beings free will and the ability to improve themselves as it has far more meaning than if they had just been made perfect by God from the beginning.

Augustinian theodicy

Augustine (354–430), another Christian bishop, philosopher and Father of the Christian Church, also put forward an influential theodicy in response to the presence of evil in the world: **the doctrine of original sin**. Augustine taught that God is not responsible for the existence of evil. He argued that evil entered the world as a consequence of humanity's 'original sin', where, according to the Bible, Adam and Eve misused their free will and disobeyed God. Augustine stated that evil is a punishment for sin. However, evil does not exist in itself but is brought into being by the absence of goodness. The continued presence of evil in the world is due to the ongoing misuse of free will by human beings. Therefore, human beings are responsible for the existence of evil, not God.

Sources of authority

The Lord is compassionate and gracious,

    slow to anger, abounding in love.

He will not always accuse,

    nor will he harbour his anger for ever (Psalms 103:8–9)

Teach me knowledge and good judgment,

    for I trust your commands.

Before I was afflicted I went astray,

    but now I obey your word.

You are good, and what you do is good;

    teach me your decrees.

Though the arrogant have smeared me with lies,

    I keep your precepts with all my heart.

Their hearts are callous and unfeeling,

    but I delight in your law.

It was good for me to be afflicted

    so that I might learn your decrees. (Psalms 119:66–71)

Can you remember?

- What does Christianity teach about the soul?
- How are the ideas of judgement and the destination of the soul linked in Christianity?
- Where do Christians believe they might go after death?
- What is the significance of 'end times' for Christians?

The story of Job

The story of Job in the Bible is often used to teach Christians how bad things can happen to good people. However, if they continue to trust in God and keep their faith, they will ultimately be rewarded for their suffering. Job is a **devout** man who lives a happy life. Satan maintains that the only reason Job worships and remains faithful to God is because he has been protected from evil and given a good life by God. Gradually everything Job cares about and all of his possessions are destroyed, although Job refuses to blame God. He remains faithful even though God seems to have forsaken or forgotten him. Eventually Job's faith and trust are rewarded by God and everything he had lost is returned to him with much more besides.

Sources of authority

In all this, Job did not sin by charging God with wrongdoing. (Job 1:22)

The Lord restored his fortunes and gave him twice as much as he had before. All his brothers and sisters and everyone who had known him before came and ate with him in his house. They comforted and consoled him over all the trouble the Lord had brought on him, and each one gave him a piece of silver and a gold ring.
(Job 42:10–17)

Coping with suffering

Christians have different ideas and beliefs about why people suffer and, the purpose (if any) of suffering. Most Christians would agree that a large amount of suffering in the world is caused by human beings who do evil things. However, this cannot explain other evil happenings, such as natural disasters. Many Christians accept that in some circumstances, suffering can lead to personal growth. They also understand that suffering can, sometimes bring out the worst in people and seem totally meaningless. In some cases, it can lead to a crisis of faith for some Christians, and cause them to doubt the existence of God.

Some Christians find comfort from suffering by helping and supporting others. Many charities have been created because of personal experience of suffering, either by individuals or those who are close to them. For example, Chad Varah founded the Samaritans as a result of the suffering he encountered while working as a Christian priest in London. The vast majority of Christians would agree that suffering provides an opportunity for people to demonstrate goodness. If there was no suffering then there would be no need for people to help or donate to others.

Generally, Christians accept that there are limitations to what human beings can fully understand or explain in regard to evil and suffering. They are reassured in the belief that, because of the suffering experienced by Jesus, God can at least understand and relate to human misery and pain. This reinforces the connection between Christians and God, who feel supported knowing that God is always with them even during the most difficult times.

Prayer is often used as a way of coping with suffering. It allows people to express their trust in God and communicate their experience directly to God. In Psalm 103, a great deal of thanks is given to God for being a constant source of compassion and forgiveness. Christians believe that God always listens to their prayers even if they are not always answered. This is because they believe that God has a plan for everyone and the ways in which God works out his plans are not always able to be understood by human beings.

Sources of authority

God is our refuge and strength,
an ever-present help in trouble.
Therefore we will not fear, though the earth give way
and the mountains fall into the heart of the sea,
though its waters roar and foam
and the mountains quake with their surging.
(Psalm 46:1–3)

Activities ?

1 Explain the difference between moral and natural evil, giving examples.

2 In groups identify and talk about the ideas mentioned in this topic to explain the origins of evil and the purpose of suffering. Write down what you think the strengths and weaknesses of each one are.

3 Write your own kind of theodicy to explain your thoughts on why there is evil in the world and what you believe to be the meaning of suffering.

Exam-style question

In this question, 3 of the marks awarded will be for your spelling, punctuation and grammar and your use of specialist terminology.

"Pain and suffering are punishments for not being faithful to God."

Evaluate this statement, considering arguments for and against. In your response you should:

- refer to Christian teachings
- refer to different Christian points of view
- reach a justified conclusion. **(15 marks)**

Exam tip

Make sure you can summarise the main reasons why some Christians might find it difficult to explain the existence of an omnibenevolent and omnipotent God when there is evil and suffering in the world.

Try to refer to different Christian theories to support your answer.

Summary

- The presence of evil and suffering in the world has always presented a challenge to Christian beliefs about God. There have been a number of different ideas, called theodicies, put forward that aim to reconcile the idea of an omnibenevolent, all-loving, and omnipotent, all-powerful, God alongside the existence of evil and suffering.

- Christians believe that God cannot be responsible for evil. Many Christians believe that evil exists because human beings have misused their free will and made wrong moral choices, which has caused suffering.

- Some Christians believe that experiencing suffering can help people to develop into better human beings. Suffering also gives people the opportunity to make good moral choices, such as helping others.

- Christians can respond to suffering in different ways but they believe it is important to keep faith in God and will often pray to God in times of difficulty.

Checkpoint

Strengthen

S1 Why might it be difficult for Christians to explain the existence of evil and suffering in the world?

S2 What are the key ideas in John Hicks' 'Vale of Soul Making' theodicy?

S3 How might Christians respond to evil and suffering?

Extend

C1 In what ways could natural evil and moral evil be connected?

C2 What are the differences between the Irenaean and the Augustinian theodicies?

C3 How might a Christian suggest the problem of evil and suffering could be solved?

Recap: Christian beliefs

The activities on the following pages will help you to reinforce your learning before you move on to the next chapter. It is important that you consolidate your knowledge about Christian teachings and beliefs at this stage as it will support your understanding of the other topics in this book, including:

- Living the Christian life
- Marriage and the family
- Matters of life and death.

It will also make preparation for your examinations much easier if you learn the information, practise exam-style questions and produce revision materials as you go along.

Recall quiz

Christian beliefs

1   When, where and how did Christianity begin and develop?
2   What are the three main Christian traditions?
3   Approximately, how many Christians are there in the world today?

The nature of God

4   What qualities do Christians believe are possessed by God?
5   Why is the Nicene Creed important to Christians?

Creation

6   What role does the Bible play in developing Christian beliefs about God?
7   Why might Christians have varying beliefs about the Creation story?

The Incarnation

8   What does the Doctrine of the Incarnation mean to Christians?

The last days of Jesus' life

9   What events took place in the last week of Jesus' life?

Atonement and salvation

10 What do Christians believe to be the purpose of Jesus' life on Earth?

Eschatology: Life after death

11 What does Christianity teach about the soul?
12 What is the significance of 'end times' for Christians?

Evil and suffering

13 Why do Christians think that God cannot be responsible for evil?
14 What reasons might Christians give for the existence of evil and suffering in the world today?

Activities ?

1 Important key terms in this chapter have been highlighted in **bold**. Collate all the key terms in this chapter and produce a glossary.

2 Design a brief for a cartoon strip, with captions, to teach younger children about the Creation story written in Genesis, Chapters 1–3.

3 What is the difference between a religious teaching and a religious belief? Explain their distinction as well as how they are connected, giving examples from Chapter 1.

4 Use the information in the Summary of learning to prepare revision materials. This could take the form of revision cards for each topic of the chapter or a concept map that notes the key ideas and learning points. Remember to:
   - use and highlight the important key terms, making sure you know what they mean
   - include relevant biblical references.

5 Discuss with a partner why some people might say that evil and suffering are God's problem.

Exam-style questions

(a) Outline three things that happen during the Christian Creation story. **(3 marks)**

(b) Explain two ways in which Jewish law underpins Christian ideas of atonement. **(4 marks)**

(c) Explain two Christian teachings about the existence of evil and suffering.

You must refer to a source of wisdom and authority. **(5 marks)**

(d) 'You can only believe in what you understand about Jesus Christ.' Evaluate this statement, considering more than one perspective. In your response you should:
   - refer to Christian teachings
   - refer to different Christian points of view
   - reach a justified conclusion. **(12 marks)**

Exam tips

- Learn and use biblical quotes that support Christian beliefs.
- Make sure that you can give examples of different points of view. Use sources of wisdom and authority to support them.
- Think carefully about what you want to say before you start responding to a question. Consider how you can back it up.

Summary

In this chapter you have learned some important Christian teachings and beliefs about:
- what God is like and where Christians get their ideas about God from
- the importance of Jesus' life on Earth
- how the universe and humanity came into being
- the consequence of sins and how human beings can make up for the things they have done wrong in their lives
- what happens to human beings when they die
- why there is evil and suffering in the world.

Extend: Christian beliefs

The Parable of the Sheep and Goats

Jesus often taught his followers using parables, which are stories used to illustrate a religious or moral lesson. Stories such as these contain symbolism rich in meaning and are easily remembered. Jesus used the parable of 'The Sheep and the Goats' to show his followers what would happen at the Last Judgement.

Activities ?

1 Read the parable of 'The Sheep and the Goats' either on your own, with a partner or in a group, and answer the questions below.

a Who do you think the King and the Father are meant to be?

b What do the sheep and goats symbolise and why are they being separated?

c Where do you think the King is referring to when he says, 'the kingdom prepared for you since the creation of the world'?

d Why do you think the kingdom is referred to as an inheritance?

e Make a list of the types of things that the sheep needed to do in order to enter the kingdom.

f What do you think the king means when he says, 'Truly I tell you, whatever you did not do for one of the least of these, you did not do for me'?

g Why were the goats sent away?

h What words are used to describe the place that the goats are sent to and where do you think it is meant to represent?

i What might Christians learn from reading the parable of 'The Sheep and the Goats'?

Source 1

The Sheep and the Goats

'When the Son of Man comes in his glory, and all the angels with him, he will sit on his glorious throne. All the nations will be gathered before him, and he will separate the people one from another as a shepherd separates the sheep from the goats. He will put the sheep on his right and the goats on his left.

'Then the King will say to those on his right, "Come, you who are blessed by my Father; take your inheritance, the kingdom prepared for you since the creation of the world. For I was hungry and you gave me something to eat, I was thirsty and you gave me something to drink, I was a stranger and you invited me in, I needed clothes and you clothed me, I was sick and you looked after me, I was in prison and you came to visit me."

'Then the righteous will answer him, "Lord, when did we see you hungry and feed you, or thirsty and give you something to drink? When did we see you a stranger and invite you in, or needing clothes and clothe you? When did we see you sick or in prison and go to visit you?"

'The King will reply, "Truly I tell you, whatever you did for one of the least of these brothers and sisters of mine, you did for me."

'Then he will say to those on his left, "Depart from me, you who are cursed, into the eternal fire prepared for the devil and his angels. For I was hungry and you gave me nothing to eat, I was thirsty and you gave me nothing to drink, I was a stranger and you did not invite me in, I needed clothes and you did not clothe me, I was sick and in prison and you did not look after me."

'They also will answer, "Lord, when did we see you hungry or thirsty or a stranger or needing clothes or sick or in prison, and did not help you?"

'He will reply, "Truly I tell you, whatever you did not do for one of the least of these, you did not do for me."

'Then they will go away to eternal punishment, but the righteous to eternal life.' (Matthew 25:31–46)

Source 2

The Apostles' Creed

I believe in God, the Father almighty,

creator of heaven and earth.

I believe in Jesus Christ, his only Son, our Lord,

who was conceived by the
Holy Spirit,

born of the Virgin Mary,

suffered under Pontius Pilate,

was crucified, died, and was buried;

he descended to the dead.

On the third day he rose again;

he ascended into heaven,

he is seated at the right hand of the Father,

and he will come to judge the living and the dead.

I believe in the Holy Spirit,

the holy catholic Church,

the communion of saints,

the forgiveness of sins,

the resurrection of the body,

and the life everlasting.

I believe in God, the Father almighty,

creator of heaven and earth.

I believe in Jesus Christ, his only Son, our Lord,

who was conceived by the Holy Spirit,

born of the Virgin Mary,

suffered under Pontius Pilate,

was crucified, died, and was buried;

he descended to the dead.

On the third day he rose again;

he ascended into heaven,

he is seated at the right hand of the Father,

and he will come to judge the living and the dead.

I believe in the Holy Spirit,

the holy catholic Church,

the communion of saints,

the resurrection of the body,

and the life everlasting.

Amen.

Activities

1. Explain what it means when the Apostles' Creed is referred to as a symbol of ecumenism.

   a. Find a copy of the Nicene Creed. Compare and contrast it with the Apostles' Creed and write a summary of what a non-Christian might learn about Christian teachings and beliefs from reading these creeds.

   b. Make a list of the reasons why some people might think that having a statement of belief, and saying it out aloud with other people from the same religion, is important.

Exam-style question

Christians believe that the parable of 'The Sheep and the Goats' sets out what they must do in order to enter the kingdom of God at the Last Judgement.

Consider what the parable is asking Christians to do and evaluate whether this is a realistic expectation for Christians today. In your response you should:

- refer to Christian teachings
- refer to different Christian points of view
- reach a justified conclusion. **(12 marks)**

Exam tip

Make sure you use the teachings of Jesus, where appropriate, to support statements about Christian attitudes, beliefs and actions.

2 Living the Christian life

Christian practices are religious activities in which Christians take part either individually or collectively. They include:

- **worship** – to show respect and devotion to God
- **prayer** – a request or expression of adoration or thanks addressed to God
- **pilgrimage** – a journey with religious or spiritual significance
- the celebration of **festivals** – a day or period of time of special importance for the followers of a particular religion, such as Christians, to remember or celebrate a religious event.

Christian practices also involve being part of a local and worldwide Church community. Christianity teaches that these practices should be a way of life. This is because Christian practices are believed to provide a framework for thinking and living that places God at the centre of Christian lives.

Some Christians argue that taking part in Christian practices:

- demonstrates obedience to God
- helps to develop faith and spiritual understanding.

Other Christians argue that taking part in religious activities is an opportunity for:

- experiencing and becoming closer to God
- connecting with the past and maintaining Christian traditions
- uniting Christians locally and throughout the world.

Christian practices can vary between denominations. However, some activities are common to many Christian Churches, for example:

- a service of worship on Sundays
- private and communal prayer
- reading and studying the Bible
- taking part in the rituals or **rites**, also known as sacraments, of baptism and the Eucharist or Holy Communion.

Most Churches have a special rite for **ordination**, becoming a leader within the church. Similarly, most practising Christians would pray and read the Bible at home on a regular basis.

Another common Christian practice would be to help others. Christians might do this by, for example:

- taking part in outreach work in their local community
- supporting Christian and other charities.

Some Christian Churches have practices that distinguish them from other denominations. For example, the Roman Catholic Church is devoted to the Virgin Mary, mother of Jesus. It is also devoted to the **veneration**, honouring, of relics and places associated with holy figures.

The Eastern Orthodox Church has many similar practices. In addition, it emphasises the role of **icons** – religious paintings of Jesus and the Saints believed to provide a connection to the spiritual world.

As well as having diverse practices, individual Christians and groups of Christians may still perform, interpret and understand common Christian practices differently. For example, a denomination called the Religious Society of Friends (Quakers) worships in complete silence, whereas other churches believe that the human voice has an important role to play in showing **devotion**, religious worship, to God.

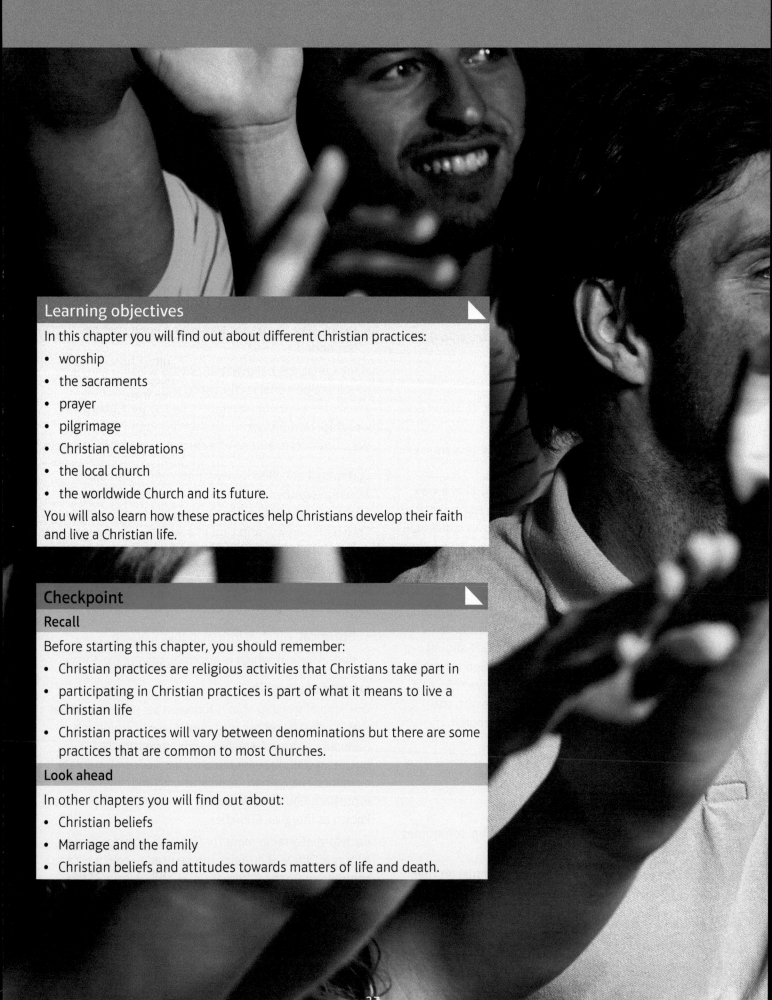

Learning objectives

In this chapter you will find out about different Christian practices:

- worship
- the sacraments
- prayer
- pilgrimage
- Christian celebrations
- the local church
- the worldwide Church and its future.

You will also learn how these practices help Christians develop their faith and live a Christian life.

Checkpoint

Recall

Before starting this chapter, you should remember:

- Christian practices are religious activities that Christians take part in
- participating in Christian practices is part of what it means to live a Christian life
- Christian practices will vary between denominations but there are some practices that are common to most Churches.

Look ahead

In other chapters you will find out about:

- Christian beliefs
- Marriage and the family
- Christian beliefs and attitudes towards matters of life and death.

2.1 Christian worship

The importance of Christian worship for Christians today

Christians believe it is very important to worship God. This is because they think that worship:

- is an expression of their faith in God
- is one way they can show their respect, devotion and thanks to God
- allows them to seek and receive forgiveness from God for the things they have done wrong
- is an opportunity for connecting with God in a way that supports and helps them to grow spiritually and understand God's purpose for them as an individual
- reminds Christians of the beliefs and traditions they share with other Christians locally and throughout the world.

However, while all Christians agree that it is important to worship God, they may have different attitudes towards the ways in which they believe God should be worshipped. Most Christians worship God through a combination of private and communal worship, and their worship is carried out in accordance with the attitudes, beliefs and traditions of their church.

Private and communal worship

Christians can worship God:

- on their own, as private worship
- with other people, as communal worship, sometimes known as collective worship.

Private worship is performed by an individual on their own, at home or elsewhere. It might include:

- meditation or reading
- trying to interpret a passage from the Bible
- silent prayer to God about things of personal concern (for example, someone they know is ill or in trouble and needs comfort or support)
- expressing thanks for something good that has happened.

Many Christians believe that private worship can help develop a personal relationship with God. Private worship is a type of worship known as **non-liturgical worship**. Non-liturgical worship does not have a prescribed form and can be carried out in different ways.

Communal or collective worship is when Christians worship together as a group. The main day on which Christians gather together to worship God is Sunday. Christians can worship God in a variety of buildings such as a private home, community centre, abbey, cathedral, citadel, minster and church. Most communal Christian worship takes place in a church. There are two types of communal worship:

- **liturgical**, which is formal, public worship
- non-liturgical, which is informal, private worship.

Liturgical worship

This kind of worship always follows a set pattern or ritual that is officially set out by a particular denomination. Generally, liturgical worship tends to be very traditional, but it can contain some more modern or contemporary elements. The Roman Catholic Church and most Protestant Churches (including the Church of England) are known as liturgical Churches.

Each formal arrangement for Christian worship is called a liturgy. Different liturgies can be used to celebrate and commemorate the different times and seasons of the Christian year. Liturgical churches publish a liturgical calendar setting out which liturgy should be used and when. The term 'liturgy' can also refer to a particular type of Eucharistic service. In Christian Orthodox churches the Eucharist service is called the **Divine Liturgy**.

Sources of authority

Liturgy refers to the patterns, forms, words and actions through which public worship is conducted. … The liturgical year provides a structure for the Church's collective memory, a way of consecrating our human experience of time in the celebration of God's work – in Christ and in human beings made holy through Christ. (The Church of England).

The times and seasons of the Christian year are symbolised by the use of liturgical colours, which are worn on the **vestments**, specially designed garments, of the clergy, and used in the hangings (material which covers some of the features in a church, like the altar) of the church building.

The 'patterns, forms, words and actions' of liturgical worship are set out in documents known as liturgical texts. The liturgical texts for the Church of England are:

- *The Book of Common Prayer* (1662)
- *Common Worship: Services and Prayers for the Church of England* (2000).

The *Book of Common Prayer* is the official service book of the Church of England and cannot be changed without Government's approval. In recent times, some Christian Churches, for example, the Church of England, have created new liturgies that reflect traditional Christian worship while using modern and contemporary language.

Liturgical churches also use a **lectionary** alongside liturgical text. A lectionary is a table of Bible readings authorised by church authorities for use during public worship. Different churches use different lectionaries, but they are all designed to ensure that as much of the Bible as possible is read during the year.

Some typical features of liturgical worship common to many Churches include:

- a procession when the clergy enter or leave the church
- formally dressed, vested clergy
- the presence of liturgical colours within the church and worn by the clergy
- singing hymns

- confession of sins and **absolution**, meaning forgiveness for wrongdoing, by the parish priest or vicar of some Christian Churches
- different kinds of set prayers
- kneeling, sitting or standing at certain times
- the reciting of the Nicene and/or the Apostles' Creed
- readings from the Bible
- liturgical readings that the **congregation**, the people in church, respond to in a set way
- **offertory**, a collection of money for charity or other worthy causes
- performing certain sacraments, for example, Baptism and the Eucharist
- sharing a sign of peace with other members of the congregation
- using incense.

Non-liturgical worship

Protestant Churches can be divided into two categories: liturgical Protestant churches and non-liturgical Christian churches. Non-liturgical Christian churches include Baptist, Evangelical, Pentecostal, and **Charismatic faith groups**; this last group is a modern movement within the Roman Catholic Church and Protestant denominations. Christians who belong to these groups believe in an experience of the Holy Spirit, which can result in healings, prophecies and **glossolalia**, known as speaking in tongues – see later. These churches do not have such an elaborate and prescribed form of worship in the same way that liturgical churches do. However, non-liturgical churches do tend to have some structure for communal worship so that that the congregation has some understanding of what is going to happen next. The important difference is that any order of service that has arisen in non-liturgical churches has developed through the custom and practices of that church and not because it has been imposed on them by a church authority. Some of the different features between liturgical and non-liturgical beliefs have also arisen as a result of different **theological** beliefs, ideas about God and religion.

Non-liturgical churches believe that Christians should be free to worship God as the Holy Spirit leads them. In Pentecostal churches and Charismatic faith groups this can often take the form of glossolalia, which is known as 'speaking in tongues': praying and speaking in an unknown language. It usually happens when someone is overcome by emotion during worship. Many Christians believe this to be a gift of the Holy Spirit.

Non-liturgical worship is mainly characterised by a lack of ritual and formality (and, in some cases, the impact of the Holy Spirit on believers during the service). For example:

- clergy do not wear special religious dress
- the Church does not practise infant baptism
- the church building is not decorated in liturgical colours.

The primary focal point in the building is the **lectern**, the stand from which the Bible is read, and the **pulpit**, the stand from which the clergy delivers a sermon. Crosses, which emphasise the risen Jesus who conquered death, are used instead of the crucifix, which can dominate in some liturgical churches.

Figure 2.1 A congregation worshipping in an Orthodox church

Typical non-liturgical worship includes:

- greater emphasis on the Bible as the inspired word of God
- a much longer **sermon**, a talk given by the clergy, than in liturgical Churches
- a Eucharist service at a table, rather than an altar
- a symbolic (rather than real) presence of Jesus in the bread and wine.

Christians who prefer liturgical worship to non-liturgical worship believe it is important to maintain the traditions of the Christian Church, many of which have their origins in early Christianity. They might also say that liturgical worship creates a more serious atmosphere, which suits the occasion better. Similarly, they could find the familiarity of the service comforting and it may give them greater confidence to take part because they know exactly what to do and when.

Some people argue there is no such thing as liturgical and non-liturgical worship; they believe there are just different degrees to which worship is organised and by whom.

Activities ?

1. In groups, discuss the significance of Christian practices for Christians today.
2. Role-play with a partner two Christians discussing why worship is an important part of their lives.
3. Design an order of service for a ceremony that celebrates or commemorates an occasion or event that is important to you.
4. Produce an information leaflet on Christian worship that could be used to educate Christians and non-Christians about the way different Christians worship and the reasons for this.

Exam-style question

Outline the key differences between liturgical, non-liturgical and charismatic worship. **(3 marks)**

Exam tip

Make sure you can describe the key features of liturgical, non-liturgical and charismatic worship, giving examples to support the points you make.

Similarities and differences between Christian and Muslim worship

Prayer is important in both Islam and Christianity as a regular form of communication with God. Both have set prayers which they may complete either as part of a service or individually. They also both have the flexibility to worship in their holy buildings or at home. However, there are fundamental differences between Christians and Muslims regarding prayer, as follows.

- Muslims perform the rak'ahs whilst praying whereas Christians tend to stay in one position, possibly with their hands together.

- Muslims face Makkah – their holy city – whilst praying. Although some Orthodox and Catholic Christians ensure they face east when praying, most Christians today are not strict about the direction they face during prayer. However, churches were traditionally built so that the altar was always aligned to the east, which does result in the congregation facing east during worship.

- Muslims and Christians both believe in One God but some Christians direct their prayers towards the Trinity. This belief that God is understood in three ways (the Father, Son and Holy Spirit) is neither understand nor accepted by Muslims.

- Although Christians may have common times to pray, they are flexible, whereas Muslims have fixed times to pray throughout the day.

- Before prayer, Muslims perform wudu, their ritual washing, which Christians do not.

Summary

- Worship is an important part of Christian life.

- Christians worship God for different reasons. They can worship God in private (personal worship) or with others (communal worship).

- There are two kinds of worship in Christianity: liturgical and non-liturgical. Personal worship is non-liturgical. Communal worship can be liturgical or non-liturgical depending on the Christian denomination.

- Liturgical worship is formal, more traditional and everything always follows a prescribed pattern.

- Some of the key features of liturgical worship are formally dressed clergy who wear different coloured vestments according to the time of year, hymns, set prayers, standing, kneeling and sitting at certain times and the reciting of the Nicene or Apostle's Creed.

- In contrast, non-liturgical worship has very few, if any, rituals or routines associated with it.

Checkpoint

Strengthen

S1 What is the difference between private and communal worship?

S2 In what ways are liturgical and non-liturgical worship different?

S3 What are some of the key features of liturgical worship?

Challenge

C1 Why might some Christians think that non-liturgical worship is more meaningful and what reasons might Christians give for preferring liturgical worship instead?

C2 How are different Christian attitudes and beliefs reflected in worship?

C3 Why might some people argue there is no such thing as liturgical and non-liturgical worship and that it is merely the different degrees to which worship is organised and by whom?

2.2 The role of the sacraments in Christian life

Learning objectives

- To understand what the term 'sacrament' means.
- To understand the role of sacraments in Christian life.
- To understand how the sacraments are celebrated in the Church of England and the Roman Catholic Church – particularly baptism and the Eucharist.

The meaning of the term 'sacrament'

Most Christian Churches, but not all, celebrate the sacraments or use the term 'sacrament'.

Christian Churches that practice the sacraments include the Church of England and the Roman Catholic Church. These Churches teach that a sacrament is an outward physical sign, established by Jesus, of an *inward*, spiritual blessing. This blessing is given to (conferred upon) a person during a special Christian ceremony, rite or ritual. These rites:

- can be conducted by the clergy privately or in public
- can take place as part of a wider ceremony, or
- can have their own dedicated service.

Christians believe that the sacramental rituals performed and prayers said express in a visible way what God is doing *invisibly*.

The role of sacraments in Christian life

Most Christians agree that sacraments:

- play an important role in Christian life
- are a way in which human beings can receive the grace, the favour and kindness, and love of God.

These Christians also think that experiencing the sacraments:

- strengthens their relationship with God
- enables them to grow in goodness and faith, and become more like Jesus
- bring additional spiritual and other responsibilities.

Christian Churches have different attitudes towards the idea of sacraments, including the number that should be celebrated.

The sacraments

Most, but not all, Protestant Churches recognise just two sacraments:

- baptism
- the Eucharist.

This is because they believe these are the only sacraments instigated or **ordained**, caused to happen, by Jesus. Some Protestant Churches also refer to

Can you remember?

- Why do Christians believe it is important for them to worship God?
- How might Christians worship God?
- What is the difference between liturgical and non-liturgical worship?

baptism and the Eucharist as ordinances instead of sacraments. According to the Bible, Jesus was baptised, at his request, in the River Jordan in Israel by his cousin John the Baptist.

The biblical accounts of the Last Supper, on which the Eucharist is based, say that Jesus initiated the meal and gave his disciples the two signs (symbols) of bread and wine, to be used in remembrance of him.

Article 25 of the 39 Articles of Religion of the Church of England (see Topic 1.6) distinguishes between what is calls the two sacraments of the gospel: baptism and Eucharist (which are believed to have been commanded by God through Jesus) and the other 'sacraments', which have not been divinely ordained.

Sources of authority

There are two Sacraments ordained of Christ our Lord in the Gospel, that is to say, Baptism, and the Supper of the Lord.

Those five commonly called Sacraments, that is to say, Confirmation, Penance, Orders, Matrimony, and extreme Unction, are not to be counted for Sacraments of the Gospel, being such as have grown partly of the corrupt following of the Apostles, partly are states of life allowed in the Scriptures; but yet have not like nature of Sacraments with Baptism, and the Lord's Supper, for that they have not any visible sign or ceremony ordained of God. (Article 25 of the 39 Articles, The Church of England)

In contrast, the Roman Catholic Church teaches that there are seven sacraments:

- baptism
- Eucharist
- confirmation
- penance, known as confession, and reconciliation
- anointing the sick, also known as **extreme unction**
- holy orders, ordination
- marriage.

Roman Catholics believe that all these sacraments:

- were instituted by Jesus and given to the Christian Church to be celebrated
- enable Christians to experience God in a variety of situations
- help to develop their relationship with God in different ways.

Baptism

Baptism is the initiation rite into the Christian faith and the Christian Church. It is considered a sacrament by most Christian Churches. Christians can be baptised as either an infant or an adult. Baptism involves making promises before God about living a Christian life. If an infant is being baptised, an adult will make these promises on their behalf.

Sources of authority

Then Jesus came from Galilee to the Jordan to be baptised by John. But John tried to deter him, saying, 'I need to be baptised by you, and do you come to me?'

Jesus replied, 'Let it be so now; it is proper for us to do this to fulfil all righteousness.' Then John consented.

As soon as Jesus was baptised, he went up out of the water. At that moment heaven was opened, and he saw the Spirit of God descending like a dove and alighting on him. And a voice from heaven said, 'This is my Son, whom I love; with him I am well pleased' (Matthew 3:13–17).

Sources of authority

And he took bread, gave thanks and broke it, and gave it to them, saying, 'This is my body given for you; do this in remembrance of me.'

In the same way, after the supper he took the cup, saying, 'This cup is the new covenant in my blood, which is poured out for you. But the hand of him who is going to betray me is with mine on the table' (Luke 22:19–21; the full version of the Last Supper, Luke 22:13–21, can be found in Chapter 1, Topic 1.4).

A key feature of baptism is water. During the ceremony, the person can have water poured over their head or they may be immersed in water. These are a physical sign of:

- cleansing
- washing away 'original sin'.

Many Christian churches, including the Roman Catholic Church and the Church of England, usually baptise people as infants. However, some Christian churches do not believe this is the best age. An alternative is the believer's baptism, also known as adult baptism. It can take place whenever a person is old enough to make decisions for themselves, which may be before the age of 18.

The Baptist and Pentecostal Churches are examples of denominations that do not baptise infants or use the term 'sacrament'.

- The Baptist Church refers to baptism as an ordinance – something ordained by Jesus.
- The Pentecostal Church focuses on the idea of a Baptism in the Spirit. This is viewed as a powerful experience. The believer is filled with the Holy Spirit, giving them strength to live a very holy life.

Another divergent Christian practice is that the Salvation Army and Quakers do not practise baptism, as they do not use sacraments.

Eucharist

The Eucharist, sometimes known as Holy Communion, is considered a sacrament by most Christians churches. It is a symbolic re-enactment of the Last Supper.

The Church of England and the Roman Catholic Church both teach that:

- the Eucharist is a rite that is both a sacrifice and a meal
- through the mystery of faith, Jesus is present during the Eucharist. His body and blood are represented by bread and wine, the physical signs of the Eucharist.

So participating in the Eucharist and receiving **consecrated**, made holy, bread and wine means that Christians:

- receive Jesus' body and blood to nourish them spiritually
- are reminded of Jesus' continued presence in their lives.

In the Church of England only Christians who have been **confirmed** can receive bread and wine during the Eucharist. Historically, **confirmation** has been seen as the second half of baptism. However, in some denominations it has now become separate from baptism.

During confirmation, an individual affirms (states) for themselves the religious promises made for them when they were baptised as an infant.

- The Roman Catholic Church considers confirmation to be a sacrament.

Figure 2.2 Consecrating bread and wine for the celebration of the Eucharist

- The Church of England does not consider confirmation to be a sacrament. However, it does regard it as a very important occasion in a Christian's life.

Christian churches that observe the Eucharist celebrate it at least once a week, normally on a Sunday. Other denominations and individual Christians may understand the Eucharist slightly differently. Some denominations, for example, the Salvation Army and Quakers, do not practise any observance of the Eucharist because they do not use sacraments.

Exam tip

Make sure you can explain what happens during baptism and the Eucharist and that you understand the meaning and significance of these practices for Christians.

Activities

1 Discuss with a partner some routines or rituals that are important in your life. Explain what these rituals mean to you.
2 Explain what you think about the Christian idea of sacraments. Give reasons for your ideas and use examples of sacraments to support them.
3 Design your own symbols to represent the sacraments of baptism and the Eucharist.

Exam-style question

Outline three features of either baptism or the Eucharist. **(3 marks)**

Summary

- A sacrament is a special ritual, associated with Jesus, during which individuals receive a blessing from God. Christians believe these blessings bring them closer to God and help them develop spiritually.
- Not all Christian denominations recognise or celebrate sacraments.
- Some Protestant denominations use the term ordinances instead of sacraments.
- The Church of England celebrates two sacraments: baptism and the Eucharist.
- The Roman Catholic Church observes seven sacraments: baptism, Eucharist, confirmation, penance and reconciliation, anointing the sick, holy orders and marriage.
- The Bible states that Jesus was baptised.
- Baptism is the rite that welcomes both infants and adults into the Christian Church.
- The Church of England and the Roman Catholic Church generally baptise people when they are babies.
- Water is used in a symbolic way during baptism. It represents cleansing and washing away of 'original sin'.
- The Eucharist reminds Christians of the Last Supper Jesus had with his disciples and the sacrifice he made by being crucified.
- Bread and wine are used as symbols to represent Jesus' body and blood.
- Christians believe that by eating and drinking the bread and wine, they are spiritually nourished through the presence of Jesus.

Checkpoint

Strengthen

S1 What is a sacrament?
S2 Why are the sacraments of baptism and the Eucharist significant for most Christians?
S3 What additional sacraments does the Roman Catholic Church celebrate?

Challenge

C1 Why do Christians have different attitudes towards sacraments?
C2 What role might sacraments play in Christian life?
C3 What do you think is the right age for people to become part of a religion and why?

2.3 The nature and purpose of prayer

Learning objectives

- To understand what prayer is.
- To understand why Christians pray.
- To understand the different types of Christian prayer.
- To understand when, where and why these prayers might be used.

Prayer

Prayer is an important part of Christian life and worship. It is a way of communicating with God. The Bible (particularly the New Testament) presents prayer as a positive thing that all Christians should do.

- Christians are urged to make time for prayer, as it will bring them closer to God.
- Prayer is shown to be a sign of faith that will be rewarded by God.
- Prayer involves talking and *listening* to God.

Sources of authority

Ask and it will be given to you; seek and you will find; knock and the door will be opened to you. For everyone who asks receives; the one who seeks finds; and to the one who knocks, the door will be opened. (Matthew 7:7–8).

Praying

Christians believe that through Jesus they can develop a personal relationship with God. One way they can do this is by praying. There are various teachings in the Bible about prayer and praying and Christians attitudes about what they believe is the best way to pray to God can vary. Christians may therefore pray to God in different ways:

- formally or informally
- in private on their own, or publically in a group
- spontaneously (on the spur of the moment), in any place at any time
- at a certain time in a set place
- aloud or silently (inside a person's head).

Prayers can be:

- very personal, and made up on the spot
- already written down or scripted, and used regularly in church (i.e. prayers which are part of a liturgy).

When Christians pray, they can use different postures (positions), for example:

- putting their hands together
- kneeling down
- closing their eyes
- sitting, standing and even lying on the floor (depending on the circumstances).

Christians pray for many reasons. One important reason is to develop their relationship with God. Other reasons include praying because they believe prayer can change things, for example, it might:

- achieve forgiveness
- heal those who are ill
- help those in need
- give people strength or courage
- create world peace
- reduce poverty
- achieve positive social or personal change.

This is known as a belief in the 'power of prayer'. Many Christians believe that miraculous things happen as a result of prayer.

While individual Christians and groups of Christians may choose to pray in different ways and for different reasons, they would all agree that the most important thing when praying is for them to have the right attitude when they pray.

And when you pray, do not be like the hypocrites, for they love to pray standing in the synagogues and on the street corners to be seen by others. Truly I tell you, they have received their reward in full. But when you pray, go into your room, close the door and pray to your Father, who is unseen. Then your Father, who sees what is done in secret, will reward you. And when you pray, do not keep on babbling like pagans, for they think they will be heard because of their many words. Do not be like them, for your Father knows what you need before you ask him. (Matthew 6:5–8)

Prayer activity is a discipline – it can be difficult at times, just like keeping fit, being on a diet, or keeping weeds down in the garden! Little and often is best, but don't give up! No prayer, however inadequate you may feel it to be, is ever wasted or of no value (The Church of England).

Our Father in heaven,

hallowed be your name,

your kingdom come,

your will be done,

on earth as it is in heaven.

Give us today our daily bread.

And forgive us our debts,

as we also have forgiven our debtors.

And lead us not into temptation,

but deliver us from the evil one.

For if you forgive other people when they sin against you, your heavenly Father will also forgive you. But if you do not forgive others their sins, your Father will not forgive your sins.

(Matthew 6:9–15)

If somebody said, give me a summary of Christian faith on the back of an envelope, the best thing to do would be to write Our Lord's Prayer (Rowan Williams, former Archbishop of Canterbury).

Types of prayer

There are many types of prayer. Christians can:

- make up their own prayers to use informally or individually, for example, arrow prayers that are used for something specific
- use prayers that have been written by other people.

The Lord's Prayer

One of the oldest, most used and best-known Christian prayers is the Lord's Prayer. Christians believe that Jesus taught this prayer to his disciples. It is formally used during most acts of Christian worship.

Prayers of adoration

Prayers of adoration praise the greatness and power of God. Those praying think about:

- how special and important God is
- all the wonderful things they believe God has done for human beings.

Christians believe that these prayers take them to a place where God is, and this enriches their soul. Formal liturgies like the Eucharist contain prayers of adoration. These prayers can also be said informally within non-liturgical churches, as well as privately.

Confessional prayers

Confessional prayers focus on:

- what it means to be a Christian
- what God expects of Christians.

Those praying think about what they have done wrong. They confess how they have fallen short of what is expected of them and ask God for forgiveness.

Christians believe that if they are truly sorry and confess their sins, God will forgive them. Confessional prayers are said as part of formal liturgies like the Eucharist, and Morning and Evening Prayer services. They can also be used more informally by non-liturgical churches and individuals during private worship.

Intercessory prayers

Intercessory prayer is when someone prays to, or pleads with, God on behalf of someone who needs help. An intercessor is someone who:

- takes the place of someone, or
- puts forward another person's case.

Christians believe that Jesus is the model for intercessory prayer. The reason they think this is because Jesus:

- put himself between God and human beings
- prayed for others while on Earth.

They believe Jesus continues to intercede from heaven for those who believe in him.

Sources of authority

For there is one God and one mediator between God and mankind, the man Christ Jesus (1 Timothy 2:5).

Intercessory prayers form part of regular everyday and weekly worship for Christians. Christian churches and groups can also set aside or nominate a complete day of prayer to raise awareness and resolve particular issues.

Prayers of petition

In prayers of petition the person praying:

- thinks about their personal needs, then
- asks God for help, guidance and sometimes forgiveness.

Prayers of petition are often said informally as part of private worship. However, some churches set aside a few moments for these prayers during their services of worship, sometimes as part of the intercessory prayers. The Athlete's Prayer is an example of a prayer of petition.

Thanksgiving prayers

Thanksgiving prayers are prayers that thank God. The person praying remembers God's love and generosity towards them and says thank you. Thanksgiving prayers can be said during corporate, private, liturgical and non-liturgical worship.

Meditation as a form of prayer

Christian meditation is another form of prayer. It is thought to be different from other kinds of non-religious meditation. Christian meditation involves focusing on specific thoughts to do with God, for example, reflecting on Jesus' life by reading or thinking about a passage from the Bible. Christians believe that the Holy Spirit helps the meditating Christian to understand God more deeply. Taize, a monastic

Figure 2.3 An athlete's prayer of petition

community, can be seen as using meditative prayer formally. Mainly, though, this kind of prayer is informal. (See Topic 2.4 for more details.)

Activities ?

1   Find your own examples of the different types of Christian prayer. Make a montage of them and annotate each one to show when, where and why they might be said.

2   In groups make a list of the people you talk to each day. Note what conversations you all have. Categorise those conversations according to what they are about. Compare your findings with the class. What do you all talk about the most? Are they the things most important to you?

3   Role-play with a partner two Christians talking about the role of prayer in their life and the different kinds of prayers they might use.

4   St Augustine said: 'Pray as though everything depended on God. Work as though everything depended upon you.' What do you think he meant by this? Note your responses and discuss them with others.

Exam-style question

Explain two reasons why Christians might have different attitudes towards prayer. **(4 marks)**

Exam tip

Make you sure can explain why some Christians might believe that certain prayers and ways of praying are better than others. Also think about what you have learnt about liturgical and non-liturgical worship and the role of prayer in private and collective worship.

Summary

- Christians believe they can communicate with God through prayer.
- Prayer is an important Christian practice. It plays a significant role in a Christian's life.
- Christian attitudes about the best way to pray can vary.
- Prayers can be said privately or communally, together with other Christians.
- They can be part of private or communal worship.
- They can be formal or informal, depending on the circumstances.
- Christians pray for many reasons in a variety of ways.
- The main forms of prayer are adoration, confession, intercession, petition, thanksgiving and meditation.
- A popular Christian prayer is the Lord's Prayer, which is found in the Gospel of Matthew 6:9–15.

Checkpoint

Strengthen

S1 What is prayer?

S2 Why might a Christian pray?

S3 What are the different types of Christian prayer?

Challenge

C1 What do you think about the idea of the 'power of prayer'?

C2 In what way could the Lord's Prayer be regarded as a summary of the Christian faith?

C3 Why might people say that prayer is a discipline like doing your homework regularly or keeping fit.

2.4 Pilgrimage

Learning objectives

- To understand the nature, history and purpose of Christian pilgrimage.
- To understand the significance of Jerusalem, Iona, Taize and Walsingham as places of Christian pilgrimage.
- To understand the importance of pilgrimage for Christians today.

The nature, history and purpose of Christian pilgrimage

A pilgrimage is a religious journey to a place that is thought to be holy or sacred. A person who goes on a pilgrimage is called a pilgrim. People make pilgrimages to:

- strengthen their faith and become closer to God
- fulfil their religious duty or show commitment to their religion
- ask for help or receive healing
- say thank you for something good that has happened
- make up for something they have done wrong (penance)
- follow tradition or satisfy their curiosity.

While 'pilgrimage' usually refers to a physical journey, the term can also mean:

- a journey through life from birth to death
- an inner journey.

An inner journey is about personal growth – the way human beings come to learn more about themselves as they grow and develop. A person's inner journey could also be a spiritual journey. Sometimes people who go on pilgrimage say they have undergone two journeys:

- a physical journey, and
- a spiritual journey.

Sometimes, Christians go on a **retreat**. This is a break from normal life for a Christian to set aside more time for God. Retreats can take place in peaceful, quiet places where Christians spend time praying and reflecting. They do this to find out more about themselves and what they believe God wants of them. These are an important part of Christian tradition.

The history of pilgrimage

Christianity has a long history of pilgrimage that can be traced back to the traditions of Judaism, which is the religion that Jesus was born into and followed.

Sources of authority

Every year Jesus' parents went to Jerusalem for the Festival of the Passover. When he was twelve years old, they went up to the festival, according to the custom. After the festival was over, while his parents were returning home, the boy Jesus stayed behind in Jerusalem, but they were unaware of it. (Luke 2:41–43)

The early Christians wanted to visit places associated with Jesus, for example:

- Bethlehem, where he was born
- Nazareth, where he grew up
- Jerusalem, where he was crucified and resurrected (see page 19).

Early Christians were persecuted, particularly by the Romans, and people who followed Christianity were mistreated and sometimes killed. This meant there were many Christian **martyrs**, which is someone who is killed for their religious or other beliefs, some of whom became saints. Early Christians wanted to travel to the tombs of Christian saints and pray there. They believed the saints were in heaven with God, and could intervene and grant their prayers (see Topic 2.3 on Intercessory prayer). The faith and courage of saints were an inspiration for Christians. Gradually the tombs of saints and other places associated with them became established places of Christian pilgrimage.

Eventually, Christianity spread throughout the Roman Empire and worldwide. As more saints were recognised, more places became important sites of Christian pilgrimage.

Jerusalem

Jerusalem, in modern-day Israel, is a popular place of pilgrimage. Israel is known as the Holy Land because it has several religious sites. Some sites are considered holy by Christians, Jews and Muslims alike. Jerusalem is important to all Christians because it is where Jesus:

- spent his last few days on Earth
- attended the Last Supper
- agonised in the Garden of Gethsemane before he was arrested
- was tried, crucified and resurrected.

Christians who go on pilgrimage to Jerusalem are able to visit many of the places where these events took place. They can also visit the Mount of Olives, where Jesus:

- taught his disciples the Lord's Prayer, and
- ascended into Heaven at the end of his time on Earth.

Many of these sites have a church built on or near where pilgrims can worship, pray or quietly reflect.

According to Christian tradition, the Church of the Holy Sepulchre in Jerusalem, also known as the Church of the Resurrection, contains two of the holiest sites in Christianity:

- the place where Jesus was crucified and died
- the location of Jesus' tomb, where he was buried and resurrected.

The Church of the Holy Sepulchre is cared for by six different Christian denominations.

Iona

Iona, an island off the west coast of Scotland, is an important place of Christian pilgrimage and retreat. It was the home of St Columba (521–597 CE), an Irish **abbot**, a Christian leader in charge of a monastery. There he established a **monastery**, where **monks** live, work and worship. Monks are men living in a religious community. St Columba is credited with spreading Christianity throughout Scotland and performing many **miracles**, extraordinary or supernatural events that go against the laws of nature.

Iona is considered a very holy and peaceful place. Its remote location gives visiting Christians a real sense of 'taking a journey'. Christians from any denomination can choose to spend time there as:

- volunteers (helping with day-to-day work)
- pilgrims on retreat
- employees.

Established members of the community do not need to spend all of their time on Iona, but they do need to follow community rules wherever they are.

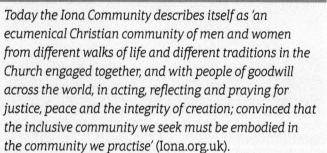

Sources of authority

Today the Iona Community describes itself as 'an ecumenical Christian community of men and women from different walks of life and different traditions in the Church engaged together, and with people of goodwill across the world, in acting, reflecting and praying for justice, peace and the integrity of creation; convinced that the inclusive community we seek must be embodied in the community we practise' (Iona.org.uk).

Taize

Taize is an ecumenical monastic community in France.

- It is made up of Protestant and Roman Catholic monks from across the world.
- It was founded in 1940 by a monk called Brother Roger as a symbol of reconciliation between different Christian denominations and other groups of separated people.
- It is popular among young people from different cultures and traditions who travel there to share in the community's way of life.
- One special experience of Taize is the **chants**, with rhythmic speaking or singing of words and sounds. Others include candle-lit services, periods of silence, Bible study and discussion groups.

A **shrine** is a place with strong, religious connotations. The shrine of Our Lady at Walsingham (in Norfolk) is the most important place of Christian pilgrimage in Britain. The shrine was built in honour of the Virgin Mary, Jesus' mother. Walsingham is the place where a lady called Richeldis de Faverches is believed to have had a vision of the Virgin Mary in 1061. Mary showed Richeldis Jesus' home in Nazareth, in Israel. Richeldis then went on to build a replica of that home.

Figure 2.4 Pilgrims kneeling for prayer in front of a shrine

Pilgrims at Walsingham pray at the Holy House and think about the Incarnation. The Holy House represents an important Christian belief that Jesus was both human and divine: Jesus was the Son of God but he also had a human mother and family.

The importance of pilgrimage for Christians today

Some Christians argue that a pilgrimage:

- is more important than ever in today's hectic lifestyles
- can help people realise how few material things they need to be happy
- can break a dependency on technologies, such as mobile phones and engaging with social media
- can set you free from the stresses and strains of everyday life and put everything into perspective.

Other Christians may not think that pilgrimage is important. They might argue that:

- it is unnecessary to go to a particular place to feel closer to God as God is omnipresent, always present, everywhere

- going on a physical journey to another place and leaving normal responsibilities behind can take away from the daily pilgrimage of Christian life (serving God and others)
- it involves needless expense, which might either place a financial burden on Christians who go on Pilgrimage or could be used to help others.

Activities ?

1. 'A pilgrimage is very different from a holiday.' Discuss this statement with a partner. Then explain to each other the place you would most like to visit and why.

2. Design an advert for a Christian retreat. Be as creative as you like. Make sure others looking at your advert can clearly find all the information they need.

3. Think why Christians might go on a pilgrimage and what you have learned about different types of Christian prayers in Topic 2.3. Write a selection of prayers that a Christian might say at a place of Christian pilgrimage.

Exam-style question

Explain two reasons why pilgrimage might be important to Christians today. **(4 marks)**

Exam tip

Makes sure you know the reasons why Christians might go on a pilgrimage. Be able to give reasons why some Christians think that modern life makes pilgrimages even more important.

Can you remember?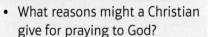

- What reasons might a Christian give for praying to God?
- Why is the Lord's Prayer important to Christians?
- What are the differences between an intercessory, confessionary and petitionary prayer?

Summary

- A pilgrimage is a religious journey to a particularly holy place. Someone who goes on a pilgrimage is called a pilgrim.
- There is a strong tradition of pilgrimage in Christianity but not all Christians agree on its importance. Christians who do think pilgrimage is important might go on one to: become closer to God, give thanks to God, make up for something they have done wrong or to ask God for healing.
- There are Christian pilgrimage sites throughout the world. Israel, also known as the Holy Land, is a popular place of pilgrimage for Christians. This is because it is the country where Jesus was born, lived, died and was resurrected.
- The Church of the Holy Sepulchre is believed to stand on the site of the two holiest places in Christianity: where Jesus was crucified; and the tomb where he was buried and resurrected.
- Other important pilgrimage sites outside of Israel include Iona in Scotland, Taize in France and Walsingham in England.

Checkpoint

Strengthen

S1 What is a pilgrimage?

S2 Why might Christians have different attitudes towards the importance of pilgrimage? Give a list of separate reasons for each point of view.

S3 Where might a Christian go on pilgrimage and why?

Challenge

C1 Why might it be more important for a Christian to go on a pilgrimage instead of a holiday?

C2 What are the holiest sites in Christianity considered to be and why are they so important to Christians?

C3 Why do you think the members of the Iona community need to follow the rules of the community even when they are not there?

2.5 Christian religious celebrations

Christmas and Easter are the two most important festivals in Christianity. They are celebrated every year and have a special place in the Christian calendar.

- The festival of Christmas remembers Jesus' birth and celebrates the Incarnation, the representation in human form of God's son. It is also a time of thanksgiving. Christians believe that, through Jesus Christ, God gave himself to the world to make things better for human beings.
- The festival of Easter takes place at the end of **Holy Week**, which consists of a series of events commemorating the last days of Jesus' life. **Easter** celebrates the Christian belief in Jesus' resurrection. A belief in the resurrection of Jesus and those who follow him is central to the Christian faith. The resurrection of Jesus is the event upon which Christianity is founded.

Extend your knowledge

Advent

Christians refer to the four weeks before Christmas as Advent, which means 'coming'. Advent is a time of spiritual preparation for Christmas, when they:

- reflect and look to the future
- think about Jesus' incarnation and what this meant for human beings
- focus on the idea of the Parousia, the Second Coming
- read passages from the Bible that recount birth (the **nativity**) and the 'coming' of the Messiah.

Other features of worship during advent and Christmas include: singing carols (hymns about Jesus' birth); advent candles and calendars, to count down the days to Christmas; a nativity scene, to represent Jesus' birth; trees decorated with lights (an important symbol of Christmas); and Eucharist, especially Midnight Mass.

Christmas

The origins of the name 'Christmas' are found in an Old English term 'Christ's **Mass**', the celebration of the Eucharist. Over time, 'Christ's Mass' was shortened to Christmas.

Christmas Day, 25 December, is the date on which the birth of Jesus is celebrated by most Christian denominations. It is also celebrated by many non-Christians worldwide and has become a public holiday in several countries. In some countries, the central focus of this festival is 24 December.

Many secular activities have grown up around this religious festival, such as a special family meal and sending Christmas cards. Jesus was God's gift to the world, which is where the tradition of giving presents at Christmas comes from.

The Gospels give an account of Jesus' birth but the actual date is not known. During the first half of the fourth century, a Roman Bishop fixed the date as 25 December. There are a number of theories why this date was chosen:

Figure 2.5 A typical Christian church altar at Christmas, surrounded by trees decorated with lights

- it was close to an existing **pagan** festival called Saturnalia, which fell the day after the winter solstice (shortest day of the year). A pagan festival celebrates religious beliefs that are not part of any of the major world religions
- it was the time of year when the Jewish religion celebrated the Festival of Lights, also known as Hannukah.

Easter

Christians celebrate Easter every year in either March or April. The date varies according to the date of the Jewish festival of Passover. This takes place on the first full moon after the spring equinox (a time when the day and night is of equal length). There is a strong connection between these two festivals because Passover is thought to have taken place between the crucifixion and resurrection of Jesus. The Gospels suggest that the Last Supper was the Passover meal.

Easter, like Christmas, is celebrated culturally (in a non-religious way) by many people throughout the world. Many people think it has pagan origins. Easter comes from an old English word 'eastre', the name of an Anglo-Saxon goddess of dawn. However, it is generally recognised as having its origins in the resurrection of Jesus Christ.

In the early Church, Easter and **Pentecost**, a festival to celebrate the Christian belief of Jesus' ascension into heaven, were the only two holy days observed by Christians. In 325 CE the Council of Nicaea formally recognised Easter as the main day of celebration. As Christianity grew, other events associated with Jesus' life became part of the Christian Church's liturgical calendar.

Another important event associated with Easter is **Lent**, a time of spiritual preparation (like Advent) over a 40-day period. It begins on **Ash Wednesday**, which is a day of repentance and humility, having a low view of self-importance compared with God. Lent is a solemn occasion for the Christian Church.

- It recalls that Jesus was tested by the Devil in the Wilderness before he began his ministry.
- Some Christians give up things they enjoy for Lent in remembrance of this.
- Others do voluntary or fundraising work.

Sources of authority

But if it is preached that Christ has been raised from the dead, how can some of you say that there is no resurrection of the dead? If there is no resurrection of the dead, then not even Christ has been raised. And if Christ has not been raised, our preaching is useless and so is your faith. More than that, we are then found to be false witnesses about God, for we have testified about God that he raised Christ from the dead. But he did not raise him if in fact the dead are not raised.

For if the dead are not raised, then Christ has not been raised either. And if Christ has not been raised, your faith is futile; you are still in your sins. Then those also who have fallen asleep in Christ are lost. If only for this life we have hope in Christ, we are of all people most to be pitied.

But Christ has indeed been raised from the dead, the first fruits of those who have fallen asleep. For since death came through a man, the resurrection of the dead comes also through a man. For as in Adam all die, so in Christ all will be made alive. But each in turn: Christ, the first fruits; then, when he comes, those who belong to him. Then the end will come, when he hands over the kingdom to God the Father after he has destroyed all dominion, authority and power. For he must reign until he has put all his enemies under his feet. The last enemy to be destroyed is death. For he "has put everything under his feet." Now when it says that "everything" has been put under him, it is clear that this does not include God himself, who put everything under Christ. When he has done this, then the Son himself will be made subject to him who put everything under him, so that God may be all in all.

Now if there is no resurrection, what will those do who are baptized for the dead? If the dead are not raised at all, why are people baptized for them? And as for us, why do we endanger ourselves every hour? I face death every day—yes, just as surely as I boast about you in Christ Jesus our Lord. If I fought wild beasts in Ephesus with no more than human hopes, what have I gained? If the dead are not raised,

"Let us eat and drink, for tomorrow we die."

Do not be misled: "Bad company corrupts good character." Come back to your senses as you ought, and stop sinning; for there are some who are ignorant of God—I say this to your shame. (1 Corinthians 15:12–34)

How Christian Churches celebrate Holy Week

- **Palm Sunday**: Holy Week begins with Jesus entering into Jerusalem – a joyful occasion and a stark contrast to the way Holy Week ended.
- **Maundy Thursday**: the day on which the Last Supper took place, when Jesus asks to be remembered through the symbols of bread and wine.
- **Good Friday**: the day on which Jesus was crucified.
- **Holy Saturday**: the last day of Lent and the day before Easter Sunday.
- **Easter Sunday**: the day on which Christians celebrate the resurrection of Jesus.

Traditionally, the Church of England and Roman Catholic Church hold a late evening service on Holy Saturday called the Easter Vigil. The word 'vigil' means 'to keep watch'.

- Worshippers who attend the Easter Vigil watch and wait for Easter Day to arrive.
- Churches are cleaned and decorated with spring flowers in preparation for Easter Day. Many churches create an Easter garden to represent the tomb where Jesus was buried.
- The service starts in semi-darkness with just enough candlelight to read the Bible.
- The church is gradually filled with more light, including the Paschal candle. This large candle represents the light of Jesus. The change from darkness to light represents the Christian belief that Jesus overcame death and enabled good to triumph over evil.

After the sadness of Good Friday, Easter Sunday is a very joyful day. Most Christians who celebrate the Eucharist will try to take part in the Eucharist celebration. Easter reminds Christians that:

- there is life after death
- with God that all things are possible.

Easter is also seen as a time of new beginnings. Many of its traditions, such as painting eggs, egg rolling and egg hunts, reflect the idea of a new life in Jesus.

Figure 2.6 The idea of the Easter Bunny bringing Easter eggs originated with the Lutheran denomination, who introduced the idea of an egg laying hare

Can you remember?

- What is the significance of the Last Supper?
- What does Holy Communion represent?
- What is the Resurrection?
- What is the Holy Spirit?
- Why are atonement and salvation important for Christians?

Activities

1. List all the traditions you associate with Christmas and Easter. State whether they are religious or secular activities. Try to find out where some of the traditions, for example, Pancake Day, have come from.
2. Explain what you can give to people instead of material gifts. List the reasons people might prefer being given non-material things.
3. In groups, discuss how the concepts of atonement, redemption, reconciliation and salvation are linked to the festivals of Christmas and Easter.

Exam-style question

Explain why the festivals of Christmas and Easter are significant for Christians. **(5 marks)**

You must refer to a source of authority in your answer.

Exam tip

Make sure you know, and can explain, with reference to a source of authority such as a quote from the Bible, the meaning and importance of Easter and Christmas to Christians.

Summary

- Christmas and Easter are the two most important Christian festivals celebrated by Christians.
- Christmas celebrates Jesus' birth and the Christian belief in the Incarnation.
- Easter remembers Jesus' crucifixion and death. It celebrates the Christian belief in the resurrection of Jesus. This is the event upon which the Christian faith is founded.
- Both of these festivals are a time for reflection. Christians think about the meaning and purpose of Jesus' life on Earth, and the significance of his crucifixion and resurrection.
- Christians prepare for Christmas during Advent. At Christmas time they will sing carols and focus on Bible readings related to Jesus' birth.
- Churches are likely to be decorated with Christmas trees and lights. They may also have a nativity scene.
- Light is an important symbol associated with Jesus who is believed to be 'the light of the world'.
- Attending a Eucharist service, either Midnight Mass on Christmas Eve or on Christmas Day, would be important to many Christians.
- Christians prepare for Easter during Lent, which is a solemn time for the Christian Church.
- At the end of Lent churches are decorated with spring flowers in preparation for Easter Sunday.
- Some Churches hold a candle-lit vigil on Easter Saturday evening and begin Easter Sunday with a bonfire at dawn.
- Churches hold a Eucharist service on Easter Sunday morning. Most Christians would try to attend.
- Eggs have become a symbol of Easter and represent new life.

Checkpoint

Strengthen

S1 What do the festivals of Easter and Christmas celebrate?

S2 How might Christians celebrate the festivals of Easter and Christmas?

S3 Why are Easter and Christmas considered to be the most important Christian festivals?

Challenge

C1 Why might Christians think about and try to help people less fortunate than themselves, particularly at Christmas time?

C2 Explain why Christians think that light is a good symbol to represent Jesus.

C3 Why is the resurrection of Jesus important to the Christian faith?

2.6 The local parish church

The local church within the parish community

A parish is a specified geographical area that has its own church and minister.

- If the parish church is Roman Catholic, the minister is called a parish priest.
- If the parish church is Church of England, the minister is called a vicar or rector.
- The parish community means everyone who lives in the local area of the church. However, not every member of a parish goes to church.

The Churches divided into parishes are:

- Church of England
- Roman Catholic
- Church of Scotland
- Church of Wales
- United Methodist Church.

Rural areas are likely to have just one church within a parish. Towns and cities designated as 'parishes' may have:

- many different Christian denominational churches
- places of worship connected with other religions.

According to the English Church Census in 2005, there were 37,501 known churches in England. The Church of England has 16,000 parish churches. Each of these is run by a vicar or rector alongside a Parochial Church Council (PCC). Anyone on the **electoral register**, a list of people entitled to vote in a district or area, can have a place on the PCC. However, the PCC is usually formed from members of the church congregation.

Sources of authority

The best English parish churches do not conform to any defined standard imposed from above. They find their place among their local community and grow out of it, imaginatively tailoring their activities to the needs of their locality (Baroness Wilcox of Plymouth, Chairman of London's Diocesan Advisory Committee).

The role and importance of the local parish church

Christians believe they have a responsibility to love their neighbour based on Jesus' teachings in the Bible (for example, Mark 12:31). For them, this means they should care for others. The Parable of the Good Samaritan (Luke 10:25–37) teaches Christians that their 'neighbour' is anyone in need. Another passage in the Bible 1 Peter 5:1–4 suggests that vicars and parish priests who are allocated to parishes as spiritual leaders have a special responsibility to lead by example, serve and care for people within that parish. They are likened to a shepherd who cares for their flock of sheep.

Sources of authority

To the elders among you, I appeal as a fellow elder and a witness of Christ's sufferings who also will share in the glory to be revealed: be shepherds of God's flock that is under your care, watching over them – not because you must, but because you are willing, as God wants you to be; not pursuing dishonest gain, but eager to serve; not lording it over those entrusted to you, but being examples to the flock. And when the Chief Shepherd appears, you will receive the crown of glory that will never fade away. (1 Peter 5:1–4.)

The parish structure means the Church is there for everyone who lives in the local community – whether they are Christians or non-Christians. The Church of England describes itself as a 'Christian presence in every community'. This includes:

- remote isolated settings
- quiet rural villages
- market towns
- busy inner cities.

The parish church is an important centre of Christian worship and identity within every community. It is:

- the focal point for Christian practices

- part of a network of Christian churches and communities across the world

Providing the parish church works in accordance with the Church's liturgical requirements, it is able to:

- make decisions about the number of services held
- choose the format of a Eucharist service.

Local churches are keen to help families (as covered in Topic 3.4). They can contribute in many other ways, too.

- Church buildings can be used as cultural venues. According to estimates, approximately half the UK's church buildings are used for arts, music and dance activities. Many people visit church buildings or places of worship to attend concerts, community events or to find somewhere quiet to think.
- The Church Urban Fund (2013) says that 54 per cent of Anglican parishes (including the Church of England) hold at least one organised activity to help with, for example, loneliness, family breakdown and poverty. Many churches run night shelters for the homeless. Some have food banks in conjunction with the Trussell Trust.

Extend your knowledge

The Church Urban Fund is the Church of England's response to poverty. Its aim is to 'inform, inspire, resource and support churches as they work to tackle poverty and build community… We take what Jesus says about loving God and loving our neighbours seriously. We are passionate about bringing God's love, hope and justice to the poorest and most marginalised people in England, empowering them to transform their lives. And we believe the local church is uniquely placed to bring lasting change to its community.'

The Church Urban Fund has identified three kinds of poverty:

- poverty of resources – when people do not have enough resources, such as income, skills, qualifications or health, to have a good lifestyle
- poverty of relationships – when people do not have strong and supportive relationships to sustain them and help them to thrive
- poverty of identity – when people do not have faith in themselves. They lack self-esteem and confidence in their own abilities.

Through the work of the Church Urban Fund, thousands of churches are working with their local communities to end poverty by providing food banks, job clubs, debt advice and night shelters.

- During natural disasters such as severe flooding in the UK, church buildings can be used as places of shelter.
- Some members of local churches act as Street or Night Pastors, particularly in city parishes. These pastors go into the local community at night to build relationships with locals. They offer a listening ear, practical support and prayer to everyone they meet.
- The local church occasionally provides support and counselling services for issues, such as drug and alcohol misuse, finance and debt, and mental health.

Running night shelters, establishing food banks and Street/Night Pastors are all examples of Christian outreach work – providing support and help for those who may not be able to get help in other places.

Another important parish activity is promoting **ecumenism**, the unity of Christian Churches throughout the world. This may use the resources of Churches Together in England (CTE), an ecumenical organisation that develops understanding and co-operation among Christian groups. In recent years, CTE has adopted an approach called **receptive ecumenism**, to be open to what different Churches can add to their own traditions.

All of these activities and provisions that take place in many parishes give Christians a centre of identity and worship through living practice.

Sources of authority

But if we love God, inasmuch as we come near to Him by love of Him, so we become united by love with our neighbours, and inasmuch as we are united with our neighbours, so we become united with God (Abba Dorotheos of Gaza).

In order to unite with one another, we must love one another; in order to love one another, we must know one another; in order to know one another, we must go and meet one another (Cardinal Mercier, c.1920).

Figure 2.7 The Churches Together in England logo portrays the Church as a ship afloat on the sea of the world with the mast in the form of a cross, itself the key symbol of the Christian Faith. The symbol of a boat is common throughout the ecumenical movement. It has been used by the World Council of Churches since 1948. Its origin is in the Gospel stories of Jesus calling Galilean fishermen and stilling the storm on Lake Galilee (Churches Together in England)

Figure 2.8 Street Pastors, listening, caring and helping

Activities ?

1. Role-play two Street/Night Pastors discussing their outreach work and why they do it.

2. Describe the three different types of poverty identified by the Church Urban Fund. Explain how local churches could help to address these issues.

3. Use the information in Topic 3.4 and in this topic to produce a diagram or written summary showing how parish churches can help their local communities.

Can you remember?

- What do the festivals of Christmas and Easter celebrate?
- How do Christians celebrate Christmas and Easter?
- Why are Christmas and Easter regarded as the two most important Christian festivals?

Exam-style question

Explain the importance of the parish church to the local community. **(5 marks)**

You must refer to a source of authority in your answer.

Exam tip

Make sure you understand, with reference to a source of authority, the ways in which local parish churches support members of the local community.

Summary

- A parish is a geographical area with its own church and parish priest, vicar or rector, who has a special responsibility to serve and care for members of the local community.
- It is the centre of Christian worship and identity within the community.
- Christians believe it is very important to help others, especially those less fortunate and who live in poverty.
- Parish churches support their local community by providing a variety of different services for individuals, families and groups. Some examples are running a counselling service, food banks, job clubs and night shelters.
- Churches also assist by giving temporary shelter and food in emergencies such as flooding.
- Christian Churches are committed to working together to help others locally and worldwide. This is called ecumenism. Churches Together in England is an ecumenical group that does this.

Checkpoint

Strengthen

S1 What is meant by the term 'parish church'?

S2 Why is the parish church considered to be an important centre for Christian worship and identity within the community?

S3 Why might members of the local community turn to their parish church?

Challenge

C1 Why do churches work to promote ecumenism?

C2 What is receptive ecumenism?

C3 What can we learn about Christian beliefs by looking at the activities of the parish church?

2.7 The worldwide Church and its future

 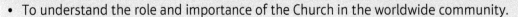
The worldwide Church

The term 'worldwide Church' literally means everyone throughout the world who follows the Christian faith. Two other terms that could also be used instead are: Christian Church and the Church.

The World Council of Churches (WCC) represents the worldwide Church, although not all Christian denominations are members of the WCC. For example, the Roman Catholic Church is not a member but it does work closely with it, sending observers to all WCC meetings.

The World Council of Churches was established in 1948. It describes itself as: 'A worldwide fellowship of 345 global, regional and sub-regional, national and local churches seeking unity, a common witness and Christian service.'

World Council of Churches

Figure 2.9 The cross and the boat, early Christian symbols of the Church, embody faith and unity. They form the logo of the World Council of Churches (WCC) and carry the message of the ecumenical movement. The word 'oikoumene' comes from the Greek word 'oikos', meaning house. Its English equivalent is 'ecumenical'. It signifies the whole household of faith, all races, all nations, all Churches

The role and importance of the Church in the worldwide community

The WCC believes the Church in the worldwide community should:

- demonstrate the essential unity of the Christian faith
- promote the Christian faith
- engage in Christian service (to be helpful to those in need – based on the idea of stewardship).

The idea of stewardship:

- comes from the accounts of Creation in the Bible
- is reinforced by Jesus' teaching that human beings will be judged by God in accordance with how they have treated others.

According to the Bible, Jesus teaches his followers to love one another.

The kind of love Jesus is referring to is agape, the main type of love featured in the Bible (see Chapter 3, Topic 3.2 for more details). Christians believe they should always do the most loving thing in any situation, even if it is difficult. 1 Corinthians 13, written by St Paul, outlines a Christian understanding of love.

Christian attitudes towards charity

The Christian concept of agape and the idea of being of service to others can be seen in Christian attitudes towards charity. Christianity teaches that everything comes from and belongs to God. Therefore, Christians should be thankful for what they have and share it with others. The Parable of the Sheep and Goats (Matthew 25:31–46, see Chapter 1 Extend) is a biblical teaching, which is often used in Christianity to remind Christians of their responsibilities towards people who are in need and the consequences of not helping others.

Sources of authority

If I speak in the tongues of men or of angels, but do not have love, I am only a resounding gong or a clanging cymbal. If I have the gift of prophecy and can fathom all mysteries and all knowledge, and if I have a faith that can move mountains, but do not have love, I am nothing. If I give all I possess to the poor and give over my body to hardship that I may boast, but do not have love, I gain nothing.

Love is patient, love is kind. It does not envy, it does not boast, it is not proud. It does not dishonour others, it is not self-seeking, it is not easily angered, it keeps no record of wrongs. Love does not delight in evil but rejoices with the truth. It always protects, always trusts, always hopes, always perseveres.

Love never fails. But where there are prophecies, they will cease; where there are tongues, they will be stilled; where there is knowledge, it will pass away. For we know in part and we prophesy in part, but when completeness comes, what is in part disappears. When I was a child, I talked like a child, I thought like a child, I reasoned like a child. When I became a man, I put the ways of childhood behind me. For now we see only a reflection as in a mirror; then we shall see face to face. Now I know in part; then I shall know fully, even as I am fully known.

And now these three remain: faith, hope and love. But the greatest of these is love. (1 Corinthians 13)

The idea of Christian charity can vary between individual Christians and groups of Christians. Some Christians believe that it is about showing love and caring for the poor and disadvantaged, whereas other Christians believe that it is about showing Jesus' love in their daily lives. All Christians would agree that they can demonstrate the love of God in a practical way by doing charitable acts.

Sources of authority

The earth is the Lord's, the Lord's and everything in it, the world, and all who live in it (Psalm 24:1).

The Bible teaches that Christians should set aside 10 per cent of their wealth for charity. This is known as **tithing**.

- Some Christians choose to do this.
- Others may give more or less than 10 per cent, depending on their circumstances.

Sources of authority

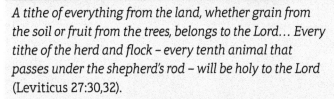

A tithe of everything from the land, whether grain from the soil or fruit from the trees, belongs to the Lord… Every tithe of the herd and flock – every tenth animal that passes under the shepherd's rod – will be holy to the Lord (Leviticus 27:30,32).

Christians believe you can also give to charity in other ways that don't involve giving money, for example:

- doing voluntary work
- doing a sponsored activity
- visiting someone who is lonely.

Christians think giving to charity selflessly and with genuine love (as in 1 Corinthians 13) is much more important than doing it just to look good. In the Bible Jesus criticises people who follow religious teachings without really caring about helping people. Christians believe God knows what is in the heart of those giving to charity and will judge them accordingly.

Christian Aid is an example of an international Christian charity that works with people of all religions and those without a belief in God in more than 50 countries throughout the world. The work of Christian Aid is founded on a strong belief in the teachings of the Gospels and is sponsored by 41 British and Irish Churches. Christian Aid works to eradicate the causes of poverty and achieve social justice. See also Chapter 3 Topic 3.8 for more information about the work of Christian Aid.

Sources of authority

Christian Aid insists the world can and must be swiftly changed to one where everyone can live a full life, free from poverty. We work globally for profound change that eradicates the causes of poverty, striving to achieve equality, dignity and freedom for all, regardless of faith or nationality (Christian Aid mission statement).

Figure 2.10 Dr David Livingstone (1813–1873) was a famous Scottish missionary doctor who spent most of his life in Africa. He wanted to stop poverty and slavery in Africa. Dr Livingstone thought that he could do this by introducing Christianity to Africa and encouraging trade with Europe

Sources of authority

O Lord God,
your Son Jesus Christ suffered and
died for us.
In his resurrection
he restores life and peace in all
creation.
Comfort, we pray, all victims of
intolerance
and those oppressed by their fellow
humans.
Remember in your kingdom those
who have died.
Lead the oppressors towards
compassion
and give hope to the suffering.
Through the same Jesus Christ our
Lord. Amen
(Church of England Prayer for the
Persecuted Church)

How and why the Church works for reconciliation

Christian service involves reconciliation – breaking down barriers:

- between people
- between people and God.

Other aspects include:

- seeking justice and peace for everyone
- working to ensure the **integrity**, which here means whole and undivided, of God's creation.

The worldwide Church believes love, forgiveness and reconciliation are important themes. It works for reconciliation because it believes it is part of the Christian mission or purpose. The Bible teaches that:

- all are one in Jesus (Galatians 3:28)
- through the peace of Jesus people who are divided can be brought together
- faith in Jesus can bring together divided individuals and groups of people.

The problems of the persecuted Church

Religious persecution is the mistreatment of an individual or groups because of their religious beliefs. Even today, Christians are discriminated against, abused and killed because of their faith. In 2016, trends showed persecution against Christians was increasing.

In some places, life as a Christian is very frightening and dangerous. Just having a copy of the Bible can lead to imprisonment or death. Persecution of Christians includes:

- open hostility towards individuals (at worst, resulting in murder)
- destroying churches and other holy sites or objects.

Some Christian organisations and individuals work hard to solve the issues of a persecuted Church. They include the WCC, Open Doors, Release International and individual Christians and Christian Churches. Similarly, non-Christian organisations working in the same way include Amnesty International and some Western governments.

The future of the Church

Church attendance in the UK is thought to be declining – especially among the young. However, current trends suggest that Christianity worldwide is growing and by 2050 Christians will number approximately 3 billion.

Historically, the Church has grown through missionary and evangelical outreach work. This is because Christians believe that Jesus commanded his followers to **evangelise**, share their beliefs with others.

Evangelism is the Christian practice of spreading the 'Good News' about Jesus: sharing the belief that salvation is possible through Jesus. The purpose of evangelism is to get people to accept Jesus Christ as their personal saviour. Once they have been converted they have a responsibility to help evangelise others. In the past, methods of evangelism were quite limited. However, in modern times people can evangelise by:

- inviting people to attend church
- having one-to-one conversations with family, friends, colleagues and acquaintances
- preaching on street corners or other open-air spaces in towns and cities
- going door to door and approaching strangers
- living their lives in a way that shows others the impact of God on their lives
- advertising (particularly at key times in the Christian year)
- speaking on radio, TV, the internet and social media
- creating Christian rock music (thought to be a very effective way of encouraging young people to find out more about Christianity).

Missionary work is a form of evangelism. Christians are sent by their Church or a missionary organisation to a particular area (usually another country), mainly to **proselytise**, to try to convert people to Christianity. Historically, missionaries were sent to parts of the world that had never heard of Jesus or the Christian faith.

According to the Bible, members of the early Christian Church, particularly Jesus' disciples, were very active missionaries. Christianity spread further when it became the official religion of the Roman Empire.

Another way Christianity has spread has been through **colonisation**, where Western European countries such as England, France, Portugal, Spain and Holland colonised and ruled other parts of the world (usually from a distance).

- This means they imposed a new way of life, including religion, on the indigenous peoples (the original inhabitants).
- It also explains why some areas of the world are associated with particular denominations, for example, the Roman Catholic tradition in South America brought in by Spanish and Portuguese Catholic explorers. Even after decolonisation, the Roman Catholic faith remained.
- Similarly, North America was colonised by the Protestant British settlers. Today the majority of Americans who are Christian are from Protestant traditions.

Missionary work today is very different from missionary work in the past. It is still an important Christian practice, but focuses much more on the provision of aid. An example of this is the work of the Church Mission Society, originally founded in 1799. Nowadays, Christians prefer to use the term 'evangelise' instead of 'proselytise' to describe their missionary work.

Sources of authority

When Jesus rose early on the first day of the week, he appeared first to Mary Magdalene, out of whom he had driven seven demons. She went and told those who had been with him and who were mourning and weeping. When they heard that Jesus was alive and that she had seen him, they did not believe it. Afterward Jesus appeared in a different form to two of them while they were walking in the country. These returned and reported it to the rest; but they did not believe them either. Later Jesus appeared to the Eleven as they were eating; he rebuked them for their lack of faith and their stubborn refusal to believe those who had seen him after he had risen. He said to them, "Go into all the world and preach the gospel to all creation. Whoever believes and is baptized will be saved, but whoever does not believe will be condemned. And these signs will accompany those who believe: In my name they will drive out demons; they will speak in new tongues; they will pick up snakes with their hands; and when they drink deadly poison, it will not hurt them at all; they will place their hands on sick people, and they will get well. "After the Lord Jesus had spoken to them, he was taken up into heaven and he sat at the right hand of God. Then the disciples went out and preached everywhere, and the Lord worked with them and confirmed his word by the signs that accompanied it. (Mark 16:9–20)

Sources of authority

Again Jesus said, "Peace be with you! As the Father has sent me, I am sending you." And with that he breathed on them and said, "Receive the Holy Spirit." (John 20:21–22)

Activities

1 In groups, discuss setting up a brand new charity for a cause that is important to you. Choose one idea and feed back to the rest of the class saying what your charity would support and why.

2 Read the passage from 1 Corinthians 13. Describe, using a single sentence, what the term 'love' means to you.

3 Explain why you think church attendance might be declining among young people and what could be done about it.

Exam-style question

In this question, 3 of the marks awarded will be for your spelling, punctuation and grammar and your use of specialist terminology.

'Christians are right to proselytise.'

Evaluate this statement considering arguments for and against what it is saying.

In your response you should:

• refer to Christian teachings
• refer to different Christian points of view
• reach a justified conclusion. **(15 marks)**

Exam tip

The exam-style question above is about the role and purpose of evangelism and missionary work, historically and today, from a Christian and other perspectives. You could also write about the idea of Christian service and charity work, which often accompanies the Christian sense of mission. Make sure you answer the question in a balanced way. Always try to use sources of authority to support what you are saying.

Summary

- Christianity is growing as a worldwide religion, although in the UK church attendance by young people is declining.
- Christians throughout the world form the worldwide Church. Many denominations are members of the World Council of Churches (WCC).
- The Christian Church believes it has an important role to play in the worldwide community, particularly through providing charitable works.
- In parts of the world, the Christian Church is persecuted.
- Evangelism and missionary activity have always been an important Christian practice. This is because Christians believe that they have a responsibility to share their faith with others in the hope that they will become Christians.

Checkpoint

Strengthen

S1 What is the Worldwide Council of Churches?

S2 How do Christians understand the role of the Church in the worldwide community?

S3 What does Christianity teach about charity?

Challenge

C1 What are the problems of the persecuted Church and how do Christians try to address this?

C2 How and why does the Church work for reconciliation?

C3 Why is evangelical work considered important to individual Christians and the Church?

Recap: Living the Christian life

Use the activities and exam-style questions on the following pages to reinforce your learning before you move onto the next chapter.

Recall quiz

Christian worship

1   What are the differences between liturgical and non-liturgical forms of worship?

The role of the sacraments in Christian life

2   What is a sacrament?

3   What is the significance of the sacraments of baptism and the Eucharist

The nature and purpose of prayer

4   What is prayer and why is it important to Christians?

5   What different kinds of prayer might Christians use and why?

Pilgrimage

6   What is a pilgrimage?

7   Why might Christians want to go on a pilgrimage, where might they visit and why?

Christian religious celebrations

8   What is the significance of Christmas and Easter for Christians?

9   How might Christians celebrate Easter and Christmas

The local parish church

10 What does the term 'local parish church' mean?

11 How can the parish church support the local community?

12 What is ecumenism?

13 What is outreach work and why might Christians be motivated to take part in it?

The worldwide Church and its future

14 What does Christianity teach about the soul?

15 What is the significance of 'end times' for Christians?

Activities

1   Produce a glossary of all the key terms in this chapter.

2   Imagine you are a Christian. Write a letter to Churches Together in England in support of ecumenism. Give reasons for your views.

3   Prepare a leaflet on the work of Christian Aid or another Christian charity of your choice. Make sure your leaflet contains a mission statement – a statement of the Christian beliefs held by that charity and how those beliefs are met in its work.

4   Use the information in the Summary of learning for each topic in this chapter to prepare revision materials. This could take the form of revision cards for each topic in this chapter or a concept map noting the key ideas and learning points. Remember to use and highlight the key terms, making sure you know what they mean. Also include relevant biblical references.

5   Design a job advert for a missionary. Explain the qualities needed and the importance of the role from a Christian perspective.

Exam-style questions

(a) Explain two reasons why the Church works for reconciliation. **(4 marks)**

(b) Outline three reasons why Easter is considered to be the most important festival for Christians. **(3 marks)**

(c) Explain two ways Christians respond to the decline in Church attendance. **(4 marks)**

In the following question, 3 of the marks awarded will be for your spelling, punctuation and grammar and your use of specialist terminology.

(d) C.S. Lewis, a famous Christian, once said: 'I pray because I can't help myself. I pray because I'm helpless. I pray because the need flows out of me all the time – waking and sleeping. It doesn't change God – it changes me.'

With reference to this quote, evaluate the role of prayer in the life of a Christian. You must refer to Christianity in your answer. **(15 marks)**

Exam tips

- Make sure you can explain the religious significance of Christian festivals, such as Easter, for Christians.

- Ensure that you know the meanings of the important Christian terms, the different ways different Christians might interpret them and why they are important to Christians.

- Make sure you can explain Christian beliefs about the role and importance of prayer, giving different examples of when and where a Christian might pray and the types of prayer they might use. Remember to refer back to the quote when answering the question.

- Make sure you can support all your explanations with appropriate quotes from sources of authority.

Summary of learning

In this chapter you have learned some important Christian teachings and beliefs about:

- the different ways that Christians can worship
- the nature of sacraments and their importance to Christians
- the nature and purpose of prayer
- the Christian festivals of Christmas and Easter
- the role and importance of the local parish church
- the role and significance of the worldwide Church and its future.

Extend: Living the Christian life

The Salvation Army is a non-liturgical Christian denomination that does not celebrate the sacraments. Members of the Salvation Army are referred to as soldiers of Jesus Christ. Soldiership is being a member of the Salvation Army.

Reading Source 1 and doing the activities that follow it, together with the other things you have learned in this chapter, will help you to answer the exam-style question at the end of this section.

Figure 2.11 The Salvation Army

Figure 2.12 A Salvation Army soldier

Source 1

A statement on baptism

After full and careful consideration of The Salvation Army's understanding of, and approach to, the sacrament of water baptism, the International Spiritual Life Commission sets out the following points regarding the relationship between our soldier enrolment and water baptism.

Only those who confess Jesus Christ as Saviour and Lord may be considered for soldiership in The Salvation Army.

Such a confession is confirmed by the gracious presence of God the Holy Spirit in the life of the believer and includes the call to discipleship.

In accepting the call to discipleship Salvationists promise to continue to be responsive to the Holy Spirit and to seek to grow in grace.

They also express publicly their desire to fulfil membership of Christ's Church on earth as soldiers of The Salvation Army.

The Salvation Army rejoices in the truth that all who are in Christ are baptised into the one body by the Holy Spirit (1 Corinthians 12:13).

It believes, in accordance with Scripture, that there is one body and one Spirit… one Lord, one faith, one baptism; one God and Father of all, who is over all and through all and in all (Ephesians 4:5–6).

The swearing-in of a soldier of The Salvation Army beneath the Trinitarian sign of the Army's flag acknowledges this truth.

It is a public response and witness to a life-changing encounter with Christ which has already taken place, as is the water baptism practised by some other Christians.

The Salvation Army acknowledges that there are many worthy ways of publicly witnessing to having been baptised into Christ's body by the Holy Spirit and expressing a desire to be his disciple.

The swearing-in of a soldier should be followed by a lifetime of continued obedient faith in Christ.

Activities ?

1 Read Source 1 and answer the following questions.

  a What does a person need to do to be considered for soldiership in the Salvation Army?

  b How is the presence of the Holy Spirit in a believer confirmed?

  c In what ways is the swearing in of a soldier under the Salvation Army Trinitarian flag compared with a water baptism?

  d What is the Salvation Army's response to other forms of baptism?

  e What should follow the swearing-in of a soldier in the Salvation Army and how might this be expressed?

2 Based on what you have read in Source 1 and what you have learned in Topic 2.1, why do you think the Salvation Army might not want acts of remembrance and celebrations to become established rituals?

Figure 2.13 A Salvation Army soldier

Exam-style question

In this question, 3 of the marks awarded will be for your spelling, punctuation and grammar and your use of specialist terminology.

'Rituals are just as important to a religion as its beliefs.' Evaluate this statement, considering more than one perspective. You must refer to Christianity in your answer. **(15 marks)**

Exam tips

- When reading examination questions make a note of any command words such as 'outline', 'state', 'describe', 'explain', 'assess', 'consider' and 'evaluate'. Make sure you know what they mean and the ways in which you are expected to answer the questions asked.

- Read exam questions carefully. Take a few moments to think about what they are asking you to do before you start writing. Take note of any key terms or phrases that appear in the question that could help you to answer it correctly.

- Do not go off at a tangent because you feel strongly about what you think it is.

- Make sure you understand the role and importance of the sacraments and sacramental ritual for some Christian churches. Ensure you understand the range of symbolism that can be used to express Christian beliefs. Remember that even the absence of something can say something!

3 Marriage and the family

Marriage is an ancient tradition that has two main forms: **monogamy** or **polygamy**. Monogamy means having one husband or wife at any time. Polygamy means having more than one husband or wife at the same time. In the UK and many other countries, monogamy is the legal form of marriage. According to UK law, couples can only get married or form a **Civil Partnership** if they meet certain legal requirements, for example, if aged over 16. Civil Partnerships can only take place between same-sex couples.

There are two legal types of marriages in the UK: non-religious and religious.

- A non-religious, or **secular**, marriage is called a **civil marriage**. These can take place between heterosexual or same-sex couples (apart from Northern Ireland).
- A religious marriage takes place in a religious building.
- To be legal, both types of marriage must be conducted by an authorised person, for example, a Christian vicar or priest for a religious marriage, or a state (government) registrar for a non-religious marriage.

Christianity teaches that marriage, also called **Holy Matrimony**, is a sacred relationship and a gift from God. Traditionally, Christian marriage is seen as being:

- one man and one woman in a very close relationship that lasts a lifetime
- the right situation to have a sexual relationship and children
- similar to the relationship between Jesus Christ and the Church – Jesus is seen as the bridegroom and the Church as his bride.

Most Christian denominations agree that marriage is very important. However, they also agree that not everyone needs to get married, for example, some people prefer to stay single.

Some Christian Churches, for example, the Catholic Church and the Eastern Orthodox Church, see marriage as a sacrament.

3.1 Marriage

Learning objectives

- To understand Christian teachings about the importance and purpose of marriage and its significance in society.
- To understand atheist and Humanist attitudes towards marriage and cohabitation.
- To understand Christian attitudes towards cohabitation.

Figure 3.1 Christian ideas of marriage are based on teachings in the Bible

Christian teachings about marriage

Christianity teaches that Christian marriage between a male and a female is a very important relationship in Christian life. Morally, they think it is the right relationship for sexual relations and children.

Getting married in a church in the presence of God is important to Christians. However, they also believe that marriage is much more than a special ceremony or day. Christians make vows during a marriage ceremony that they believe are sacred and binding. They promise

to live life together and treat each other according to Christian principles.

Christian beliefs about marriage are based mainly on the teachings of Jesus in the New Testament. He taught that marriage between one man and one woman was:

- part of God's plan
- what God had intended for human beings when they were created.

Christians believe that marriage is a gift from God. However, they do not think that everyone should be married in order to live a Christian life. Jesus taught that people may be single because they are doing God's work. The most important thing for Christians is that they live their life according to what they believe to be God's will. This means a single person should be **celibate**, which is someone who chooses to not be sexually active and a husband and wife should be faithful to each other.

Many Christians believe that the relationship of marriage can be compared to the relationship between Jesus and the Christian Church. Some Christians also argue that the Jesus–Church relationship is a model for all Christian marriages. Other Christians argue against this because it is based on a passage in the Bible (Ephesians 5:21–6), which they believe encourages inequality between husbands and wives.

The importance of marriage in society

Throughout the last century, attitudes towards marriage have changed and the number of people getting married has decreased. There have been a number of reasons for this, such as the decline of religious

Sources of authority

But at the beginning of creation God 'made them male and female'. For this reason a man will leave his father and mother and be united to his wife, and the two will become one flesh. So they are no longer two, but one flesh. Therefore what God has joined together, let no one separate (Mark 10:6–9)

Sources of authority

That is why a man leaves his father and mother and is united to his wife, and they become one flesh (Genesis 2:24).

influence in society; the changing status and role of women; the availability of contraception; and less strict divorce laws. These factors have led to changing social attitudes and marriage is no longer seen as the norm. In modern society, where there are an increasing number of cohabiting couples, people have different attitudes towards the importance of marriage for a relationship and its significance for society. Some people argue that marriage is no guarantee of a happy relationship or a better society.

Christians, however, argue that marriage is important for society. They believe a Christian marriage helps to stabilise society and provides a basis for good moral and social behaviour. Christians might think this for different reasons, such as:

- regulating sexual behaviour.
- providing a permanent and stable environment to have and bring up children according to Christian principles
- teaching people to be less self-centred and selfish because they have made a commitment to God and their spouse to live their married life in the way that God wants.

Not every married person is Christian or even religious. Atheists, for example, hold personal views about whether marriage is important to society. Those who agree that it is important would not do so for religious reasons.

The Humanist attitude towards marriage

The term **Humanist** is used today to describe someone who is not religious but who wants to live a good life according to the principle of reason. The principle of reason is the ability humans have to think and work things out for themselves without any belief in a supernatural being or phenomenon. For example, a Humanist would believe that science has explained how the universe came into existence.

Humanists believe in:

- shared human values and respect for others
- working together to improve the quality of life for everyone to make the world a fairer place
- marriage as a secular tradition
- marking important events like a wedding with a personalised ceremony.

Humanists do not believe in:

- marriage as a religious institution
- marriage as something established by God.

People who want to have a non-religious wedding can have a Humanist wedding ceremony. However, this would not be recognised legally in England, Wales and Northern Ireland, and couples often have a civil ceremony beforehand at a registry office.

The British Humanist Association is campaigning for the right to conduct legal wedding ceremonies for both heterosexual and same-sex couples.

Cohabitation

Cohabitation describes the relationship that two people have if they live together and have a sexual relationship, but are not married. Some Christian denominations like the Roman Catholic Church completely disagree with cohabitation. According to the teachings of the Roman Catholic Church:

- living together and having sexual relations outside of marriage is a sin
- couples who live together are not allowed to take part in Communion, like divorced or remarried people.

Other Protestant traditions like the Church of England accept that:

- attitudes towards marriage have changed
- couples live together without being married, although they hope these couples will eventually get married in a church.

The Church of England is keen to see a change in the law that ensures people who are not married are not legally disadvantaged.

Exam-style question

Outline three Christian beliefs about marriage.
(3 marks)

Exam tip

Make sure you learn and can recall different Christian and non-religious attitudes towards marriage and cohabitation.

Activities

1 Imagine you are working for the Christian magazine *Families First*. Write an article explaining why marriage is important to Christians.

2 Working with a partner, act out a role-play between two different types of Christians discussing their beliefs about cohabitation.

3 In groups, discuss the wedding vows Christians make when they get married. Summarise what you think the vows would mean in terms of their day-to-day relationship, giving examples to support your statements.

Extend your knowledge

In modern society:

- marriage is just one option for people in committed relationships
- there is wider acceptance of sexual activity and the use of contraception
- couples may choose to marry later or not at all, and decide not to have children
- divorce does not carry the same stigma
- there are higher numbers of financially independent women and people who choose to stay single
- polygamy, **homosexuality** and **same-sex relationships** are different ways in which some people choose to have relationships.

The Church of England feels that:

- marriage is very important for a healthy society and bringing up children, but
- couples who are not married should be protected by new laws.

Christian relationships such as marriage are explored in the Trinity and the biblical idea of a **covenant**, a legal agreement.

Summary

- Christians believe that marriage is:
  - part of God's plan for many, but not all, human beings; it is a gift from God
  - a lifelong, monogamous relationship, between one man and one woman
  - the right relationship for sexual relations and having children.
- Christianity teaches that single people should live a celibate life and that cohabitation is a sin. However, individual Christians and groups of Christians can have different views on this.
- Non-religious people may or may not agree with marriage, depending on their personal beliefs. A Humanist wedding ceremony is becoming more popular as a secular alternative.

Checkpoint

Strengthen

S1 Why do Christians believe marriage is important?

S2 What does getting married in a church mean to Christians?

S3 In what ways do Christians think that marriage benefits society?

Challenge

C1 Why might individual Christians and groups of Christians have different attitudes towards cohabitation?

C2 Why do you think Humanist weddings are becoming more popular?

C3 What reasons might a person have for choosing to be celibate?

3.2 Sexual relationships

Learning objectives

- To understand Christian teachings about sexual relationships.
- To understand atheist and Humanist attitudes towards sexual relationships.

Christian teachings about sexual relationships

Christianity teaches that sexual relationships should only take place between a man and a woman who are married to each other. The Bible says throughout that:

- sex should only take place within marriage and that all other forms of sexual activity are forbidden
- marriage should be respected, and the sexual relationship between a husband and wife should be kept pure
- after death, God will judge and punish people who commit adultery and those who are sexually immoral.

Christian attitudes towards sexual relationships can vary. Some Christians agree with these points. They think sex before marriage, adultery, prostitution and homosexual relationships are wrong, as highlighted in 1 Corinthians 6:7–20, for example. They think these kinds of sexual relationships disrespect the human body which, according to the Bible, is the 'temple of the Holy Spirit' and belongs to God. The purity ring (**Figure 3.2**) is how some Christians choose to show their views on sexual purity.

Figure 3.2 The purity ring is a modern idea that began in the USA. This ring is worn on the third finger of the left hand by a teenager or adult to show they have made a commitment to remain sexually pure and not have sex until they are married

Sources of authority

Marriage should be honoured by all, and the marriage bed kept pure, for God will judge the adulterer and all the sexually immoral (Hebrews 13:4).

But the cowardly, the unbelieving, the vile, the murderers, the sexually immoral, those who practice magic arts, the idolaters and all liars – they will be consigned to the fiery lake of burning sulfur. This is the second death (Revelation 21:8).

Sources of authority

Flee from sexual immorality. All other sins a person commits are outside the body, but whoever sins sexually, sins against their own body. Do you not know that your bodies are temples of the Holy Spirit, who is in you, whom you have received from God? You are not your own; you were bought at a price. Therefore honour God with your bodies (1 Corinthians 6:18–20).

Can you remember?

- What does Christianity teach about marriage?
- Why do Christians believe that marriage is important for society?
- What is the Humanist attitude towards marriage?

Two Christian views on sexual relations

View 1: Some Christians argue the main purpose of sex within marriage is to have children. This means sex should only take place between a man and a woman, as same-sex couples cannot naturally produce a child. Christians base this belief on a biblical command from the Creation in Genesis 1:28. This says human beings are to be 'fruitful and increase in number'. Other Christians say that sex between a husband and wife has another

Figure 3.3 Christianity teaches that having children is one of the main reasons for sexual relationships

purpose: it is an important expression of their love and unites them as a couple. This comes from Genesis 2:24, which refers to a man and a woman being united in 'one flesh'.

View 2: Some Christians think the attitudes in View 1 are outdated. They would argue that Christianity is about **agape** (selfless, unconditional love). They think it is wrong to criticise sex in a relationship that is committed and loving, even if those involved are cohabiting rather than married. This means some Christians might also find sexual relationships between homosexuals acceptable within a permanent and caring relationship. Christians disagree with people having sex within casual or short-term relationships.

Atheist and Humanist attitudes towards sexual relationships

Depending on their personal views, atheists may have differing opinions about:

- some sexual activities
- sex outside of marriage
- adultery
- prostitution
- homosexuality.

Their views would not be based on religious teachings.

Freedom and choice are two important Humanist values, providing they do not cause harm to anyone else. Humanists believe consenting adults should be free to have the sexual relationships they want as long as those relationships do not damage others. Humanists are opposed to all forms of sexual abuse and exploitation. As with any choice made by human beings, Humanists believe people should think about the consequences of their sexual relationships, making responsible and thoughtful choices that take into account the happiness of those involved.

Exam-style question

Explain two different Christian attitudes towards sexual relationships. **(4 marks)**

Exam tip

It is important to remember that while there are strict teachings about sexual relationships in Christianity (mainly from the Bible), different denominations and individual Christians can have different views.

Activities ?

1   Discuss with a partner what you think about Christian and Humanist ideas about sexual relationships.

2   Draw a series of flowcharts or another kind of diagram showing the different Christian attitudes and the Humanist attitude towards sexual relationships.

3   Explain why some Christians might say that Christianity is a religion of love. Outline how this might influence attitudes towards sexual relationships.

Extend your knowledge

Some people say there are four types of love for Christians to understand. This is because the New Testament was originally written in a form of Greek, which used different words to describe different kinds of love.

- The main type of love featured in the Bible is agape. This is a non-sexual, unconditional, self-sacrificing love shown by God and Jesus that all Christians are to emulate. Agape is more of an action than a feeling and is sometimes difficult to achieve. For example, a mother who stays up all night to look after a sick child, even though she may be exhausted, demonstrates agape. Christians believe they should always do the most loving thing in any situation despite their own difficulties.
- The term **philia** refers to platonic love – a strong liking or friendship. This type of love describes a positive and close connection.
- **Storge**, another platonic type of love, is used to describe the love that exists between parents and children. It also describes the kind of love between siblings or a married couple.
- Finally, there is **eros**, a sexual or passionate love. Many Christians might agree that a good marriage is based on all four kinds of love.

Summary

- The Bible has strict teachings about sexual relationships, and some Christians believe God will punish sexual immorality.
- Some Christians believe sex should only take place between a man and a woman within marriage.
- Others have a more liberal view but only if a couple are in a committed and loving relationship.
- Atheist views about sexual relationships differ according to personal beliefs.
- Humanists think sexual relationships are a matter of personal choice, as long as everyone involved is happy with those choices.

Checkpoint

Strengthen

S1 What does Christianity teach about sexual relationships?

S2 How does the wearing of a purity ring by some Christians reflect their beliefs?

S3 What is the Humanist attitude towards sexual relationships?

Challenge

C1 Why do you think Christians could have different attitudes towards sexual relationships?

C2 How are the Humanist values of freedom and choice reflected in their attitude towards sexual relationships?

C3 Why might Christians disagree with the Humanist attitude towards sexual relationships?

3.3 Families

Different types of family

Family structures within society have changed over the last 50 years. There has been a significant increase in the number of single parent, step or blended families, cohabiting couples, same-sex couples and grown-up children living at home for longer. As a result, there is now a wide range of family structures in modern society, as explained below.

Nuclear family

The traditional definition of the nuclear family is a unit that consists of a male and a female parent who are married to each other, plus their children. These days, the definition of a nuclear family also includes cohabiting couples and their children.

Single-parent family

A single-parent family refers to a person, male or female, who has a dependent child or children but is unmarried, divorced or widowed.

Same-sex family

In a same-sex family two people of the same sex live together, with or without children, either as a married couple or cohabiting.

Extended family

An extended family is a unit that goes beyond the nuclear family to include several generations such as grandparents, aunts, uncles and cousins. Extended families live close to each other or in the same household.

Blended family

The blended family, sometimes also known as a stepfamily or a reconstituted family, includes children from the previous marriages or relationships of either the husband or wife, or both.

Figure 3.4 A blended family

Modern society has many family types, but the nuclear family structure remains the norm for most people in the UK.

Christian teaching and beliefs about the importance and purpose of the family

Christians believe the family was established by God during Creation and that marriage is the right relationship within which to have children. Many

Sources of authority

The gift of marriage brings husband and wife together in the delight and tenderness of sexual union and joyful commitment to the end of their lives.

It is given as the foundation of family life in which children are [born and] nurtured and in which each member of the family, in good times and in bad, may find strength, companionship and comfort, and grow to maturity in love (Book of Common Prayer, Church of England Marriage Ceremony).

Children are a heritage from the Lord, offspring a reward from him (Psalms 127:3).

Source

The Church of England says:

The family remains the most important grouping human beings have ever developed. Children thrive, grow and develop within the love and safeguarding of a family. Within the family we care for the young, the old and those with caring needs. Families should be able to offer each of their members commitment, fun, love, companionship and security. (churchofengland. org, 2010)

Christians believe they have a responsibility to have children, if they are able to. The Bible also teaches that children are a blessing from God.

In modern society Christian families come in many forms. There is a belief these families have an important role in society and within the Church. Christians and non-Christians alike see the family as a building block of society. This is because the family is where children are cared for, learn moral values and are taught the ways of society. In turn, these things reflect their behaviour in society.

What distinguishes a Christian family from a non-Christian family is that children will also learn about the Christian faith and what it means to be a Christian. Christians see parallels between:

- their physical family
- the family they are born into
- the spiritual family they are 'born again' into when they accept Jesus Christ as their saviour.

Many Christian parents choose to have their children baptised when they are young to show they are

Sources of authority

Children, obey your parents in the Lord, for this is right. 'Honour your father and mother'– which is the first commandment with a promise – 'so that it may go well with you and that you may enjoy long life on the earth.'

Fathers, do not exasperate your children; instead, bring them up in the training and instruction of the Lord. (Ephesians 6:1–4)

Sources of authority

Parents, do not exasperate your children; instead, bring them up in the training and instruction of the Lord (Ephesians 6:4).

Parents, do not embitter your children, or they will become discouraged (Colossians 3:21).

members of the Christian family, the Church. Other Christians from denominations that do not practise infant baptism might have a **Ceremony of Dedication** instead. A Ceremony of Dedication is where a child is presented to the congregation and vows are made to raise them as a Christian.

The Bible teaches that children should:

- obey their parents
- honour their parents
- care for their parents.

Many Christians understand this to mean that children should obey their parents until they reach adulthood, but that the responsibility to honour and care for their parents lasts a lifetime.

The Bible also says that parents should not exasperate (annoy or 'wind up') or embitter (alienate or disillusion) their children, but bring them up in the way that God wants.

Christian parents have a responsibility to love, care for, guide, support and keep their children safe, as do non-religious parents. However, they also have an obligation to teach their children about the Christian faith and bring them up as Christians. This means helping them to:

- know and understand God
- follow Christian teachings
- fulfil the purpose God might have for them.

Non-religious responses to the purpose of the family

Humanists welcome the diversity of family structures that exist today because this makes it possible for people to have the type of family that is right for them.

Source

The Humanist view would be that a family is any unit committed to sharing resources and to mutual support that defines itself as such, and that the details of family arrangements hardly matter, as long as the adults are making responsible choices and everyone involved is reasonably happy. But it would be wrong if family arrangements make some members of the family miserable or are clearly unjust or cruel (for example harsh physical or psychological punishment of children, boys being given a better education than girls, or children forced to marry against their will) (British Humanist Association).

Humanists believe that close, loving and stable relationships are important for bringing up children. They think marriage can help to support this but there are other considerations too, such as whether people can afford to have children or whether they can give their children the care and attention they need.

Humanists prefer not to follow religious or other guidelines.

Other non-religious groups, such as atheists and Humanists, may hold a range of views about:

- the different family structures that exist today
- the purpose of the family and its importance to society.

On a personal level they would not believe that children are a blessing from God and that family is the place for the passing on of religious beliefs and traditions, as they do not believe in God.

Activities

1. Discuss with a partner why it might be important for children to be taught within the family how to behave in society. Give examples to support your statements.
2. Explain what you think the purpose of the family is.
3. Describe the things Christian parents might do to teach their children about the Christian faith and encourage them to follow it.

Exam-style question

Explain two reasons why a Christian upbringing might lead to a belief in God. **(4 marks)**

Exam tip

Ensure you understand the ways in which a Christian upbringing might be different to a non-religious childhood.

Summary

- These days, there are many kinds of family structure in the UK.
- Christian families also come in various shapes and sizes and they believe that:
  - the family is important for society and the Christian faith
  - parents and children have responsibilities towards each other
  - children must obey and respect their parents
  - parents must look after their children, keep them safe and bring them up as Christians
  - the Christian family is one of the main ways children learn about the Christian faith.
- Humanists do not believe in God and do not agree with the idea of families teaching children to be religious. Humanists believe that:
  - the overall happiness of the family is more important than the structure of the family unit
  - parents should bring up their children to be caring and reasonable people.

Checkpoint

Strengthen

S1 What are the different types of family that exist in modern society?

S2 Why do Christians believe the family is important?

S3 What is the Humanist attitude towards the family?

Challenge

C1 Why do you think family structure has changed over the last 50 years?

C2 What do you think the phrase 'children are a blessing from God' means?

C3 What challenges do you think Christian parents might face bringing up children today?

3.4 Support for families in the local parish

The local parish

The Christian Church is divided into many groups or denominations, for example:

- the Church of England
- the Roman Catholic Church
- the Methodist Church
- the Baptist Church.

Denominations contain separate churches grouped according to geographical area. These are known as **dioceses**. Each diocese has smaller areas known as **parishes** or local church communities. Each parish has a priest who is responsible for Christian worship and **pastoral care**, providing emotional, spiritual and physical support and help for problems, in that parish. In smaller communities a priest may be responsible for several churches and parishes.

Sources of authority

A new command I give you: Love one another. As I have loved you, so you must love one another. By this everyone will know that you are my disciples, if you love one another (John 13:34–5).

How and why the local church community supports families

Being a Christian does not guarantee an easy life. Christians believe that part of what it means to be a Christian is to help and care for others.

Christians believe that:

- God's love can be expressed in the way humans relate to and care for each other
- they have a responsibility to care for their family and those within the 'family' of their local church.

Parishes try to support Christian and non-Christian families depending on their resources. Most churches have a website that shows what is available. Some parishes also have a Facebook page and a Twitter account.

Sources of authority

All children are welcome at St Cross Church, and we aim to include them from the time of their baptism, up to when they can take a fuller part in the worship – whether delivering a reading, or serving at the altar
(Parish of St. Faith).

Family worship

Local churches hold family friendly services so that families can worship God together. This might include:

- running a slightly shorter service
- getting children involved in worship
- providing toys for children to play with in church.

In recent times, some parishes worldwide have introduced a new, popular and fun form of family worship called Messy Church. This was founded in 2004 by a group who thought the Church wasn't doing enough to encourage local families. The group wanted to do something that would help families develop their faith together in a long-lasting way.

Rites of passage

Families often turn to their local church at significant moments in their lives such as the birth of a child, a marriage or the death of a loved one. These moments, known as rites of passage, are acknowledged through ceremonies such as baptisms, weddings and funerals. The local church will offer appropriate guidance, support and comfort at these important times. The wider 'family' of the church community will also share the joys and sorrows of these events.

Classes for adults and parents

Some Christian parents feel the spiritual development of their children can be a challenge in today's modern society. Some parishes run specific Christian parenting classes, like the Scripture Union 'Survival Skills for Parents' course to support parents in bringing up their children as Christians. Christian parents and other adults might also choose to attend other groups and classes run by their local church.

Figure 3.5 Christians encourage children to learn about the faith from an early age

- A parish might organise study and prayer groups to help adults learn more about their faith and share their experiences and beliefs.
- A parish might hold a lecture or talk on a specific topic, religious or secular. Visiting speakers from Christian and non-Christian charities often come to local church communities to talk about their work. Charity coffee mornings are a popular way of bringing people from the local community together in aid of a good cause.
- Some parishes might run courses for non-Christians to learn about the Christian faith, for example, 'Alpha', which introduces the basics of the Christian faith through a series of talks and discussions.
- Many local churches host social events such as lunch or supper clubs, activities days and weekends away. Christian parents might share their parenting experiences and receive support at these informal events, as well as in a more organised environment.

Children's groups run by local churches

The Bible teaches Christians that it is important that children learn about Jesus and the Christian faith from an early age.

Many children from Christian families attend a group traditionally known as Sunday school while their parents are in church. In some parishes, Sunday schools are known by a different names such as 'TOTs' or 'Children's club'. Typically, the content is connected with the main themes of the adult service. Churches might also:

- run baby and toddler groups like 'Bumps and babies'
- run weekday playgroups for pre-school children
- run youth groups for older children
- have links with local schools where they will deliver assemblies
- hold special services in church for schoolchildren.

Counselling

Families or individuals can talk to their local priest or another member of the parish pastoral team about things that are bothering them. Some parishes may offer specific Christian counselling services. Christian counselling is different from traditional counselling because it integrates psychology with the principles and values of the Christian faith. The aim of the counselling is to:

- help the body, mind and soul of a person
- give individuals a renewed sense of hope and optimism in their lives through having a faith in Jesus.

> **Sources of authority**
>
> *Then people brought little children to Jesus for him to place his hands on them and pray for them. But the disciples rebuked them. Jesus said, 'Let the little children come to me, and do not hinder them, for the kingdom of heaven belongs to such as these.'* (Matthew 19:14)

> **Can you remember?**
>
> - What different types of family structures are there in 21st-century society?
> - What does Christianity teach about the family?
> - What do Christians believe is the purpose of a Christian family?

The importance of the support of the local church for families today

Many Christians say that the support of the Christian Church is very important for families. Through local churches, and worldwide, it provides practical, emotional and spiritual support that helps families to thrive and develop their faith. They would also say that supporting families is another demonstration of God's love. It builds a sense of Christian community and strengthens the Church. Faith can also be strengthened through worshipping and socialising with other Christians who share the same values and beliefs.

The Christian Church is sometimes described as a loving Mother who wants to care for her 'sons and daughters' (adults and children), so they each grow and become the person God wants them to be. Some Christians say 'a family who prays together stays together'.

Activities ?

1 Design a poster advertising the ways in which a local church community could support families.
2 In pairs, plan a family activity or event that a local church could hold to support families, explaining why you have chosen it.
3 'Families should support themselves.' Discuss this statement in groups. Give reasons for and against this statement and consider how a Christian might respond.

Exam-style question

Explain two reasons, giving examples, why the support of the local church might be important for families. **(4 marks)**

Exam tip

Make sure you know the various ways in which a local church might support families and can explain why it is important for the church to do this.

Summary

- Christians believe they have a responsibility to care for, and help, others – particularly the family.
- Local churches provide both pastoral and spiritual care. They try to help families in their parish in a variety of ways, including:
  - opportunities for families to worship and develop their faith together
  - running separate children's groups or clubs including Sunday schools, and adult classes and activities
  - supporting families through the different life stages, for example, births, marriages and deaths
  - offering counselling to help them resolve problems
  - giving support as a way of showing God's love; helping families also makes the Church stronger.

Checkpoint

Strengthen

S1 How are different denominations of the Christian Church organised on a geographical basis?
S2 What kinds of support might a local church offer families?
S3 Why might the support of a local church be important to families?

Challenge

C1 What kinds of support do you think a Christian family might need in today's society and why?
C2 Why might people say that families should support themselves instead of relying on other people?
C3 In what ways might Christians say that the Church is like a 'loving Mother'?

3.5 Contraception

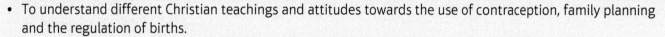

- To understand different Christian teachings and attitudes towards the use of contraception, family planning and the regulation of births.
- To understand atheist and Humanist views about family planning and Christian responses to them.

Christian teaching and attitudes towards family planning and the regulation of births

Often, Christians do not refer to the Bible when looking at teachings about contraception. Although the Bible is clear that human beings have a responsibility to **procreate**, have children, modern forms of contraception were not available in biblical times. Christian attitudes towards contraception and family planning and the regulation of births are therefore based on Church teachings, which can vary between denominations.

- All Churches disagreed with artificial forms of contraception until the start of the 20th century, but then attitudes began to change.
- Since 1958 the Church of England has accepted that parents should decide how many children they have if the contraception used is chosen by both husband and wife.
- Some people wanted smaller families so their children could have a better quality of life and success.
- The Church of England does not think contraception is a sin or goes against God's purpose. It also accepts that many **Anglicans**, people who follow the teachings of the Church of England, use contraception as a way of life.
- Other Protestant Churches share this view. For example, the Methodist Church believes that using contraception in a responsible way can bring greater fulfilment to a marriage. It thinks it is helpful in planning children (and the gaps between them) and, in some cases, avoiding pregnancy altogether (particularly for medical reasons).

Humanae Vitae

The Roman Catholic Church disagrees with all artificial forms of contraception.

- This attitude was set out in the 1930s by Pope Pius XI. He taught that artificial birth control was an abuse of the 'law of God and nature' and that those who used it sinned against God by committing 'a deed which is shameful and intrinsically vicious'.
- In 1968 by Pope Paul VI agreed with this view in the **Humanae Vitae**, which is Latin for 'Of Human Life'. He knew this document would be controversial, but he felt the Catholic Church should point out what it thought were the dangers of contraception for both the Church and society.

The Roman Catholic Church teaches that God designed sex for married men and women for the purpose of reproduction. It refers to this as a 'natural law' because it is an unchanging moral principle that all human beings should adhere to. It also teaches that:

- all marital sex must be open to conception
- using contraception is taking away the possibility of creating new life
- using contraception might make people more immoral because they may prefer sex to love; it could also mean human beings are seen as sex objects.

The Roman Catholic Church also strongly opposes:

- contraception that kills a fertilised egg, for example, the morning-after pill, because it believes this destroys a human life
- abortion, which it sees as murder.

Not all Catholics follow the teachings of the Roman Catholic Church regarding contraception. Aid agencies in developing countries, for example, have heavily criticised its attitudes. They say responsible use of contraception could:

- help to control the population explosion
- reduce poverty
- lower the risk of some health issues, such as the transmission of AIDS or the effects of the Zika virus.

Atheist and Humanist views towards contraception and family planning

Humanists have played an important role in the promotion of the use of contraception in modern times. They do not think contraception in itself is a moral or ethical issue. They agree or disagree with its use according to whether the outcomes of using contraception are good or bad.

What Humanists agree with

- They generally agree with the use of contraception, providing there are no negative consequences. The British Humanist Association thinks if contraception means every child is wanted and women are healthier, then it must be a good thing. It also suggests that the responsible use of contraception could reduce the number of abortions.
- They agree contraception should be used responsibly and should not promote promiscuity.

Sources of authority

It is best, of course, if every child is a wanted child and improved Sex and Relationships Education (SRE), more widely and freely available contraception, and better education and services for young people can all help to reduce the number of unwanted pregnancies
(British Humanist Association).

What Humanists disagree with

- Humanists disagree with the Roman Catholic Church's 'natural law' argument because they do not believe in God or God-given moral principles.

Other atheists may differ in views on the use of contraception depending on their personal beliefs. Some atheists argue that human reproductive rights are an issue that should concern everyone, whether they are religious or not.

Christian responses to atheist and Humanist views about family planning.

The Roman Catholic Church would disagree with Humanist views on contraception as they disagree with all forms of artificial contraception. The Church of England would agree with the Humanist view that the use of contraception must be used responsibly, not promote promiscuity and have a positive outcome. The Church of England and Humanists are also aligned in their hope that the appropriate use of contraception could reduce the number of abortions.

Many Christians would agree with the Humanist belief that it is best if every child is a wanted child. Some Christians might disagree with this because they believe God has a plan for everyone who is born and that what God has planned for a person is more important.

Christian Churches and individual Christians may or may not agree with atheist views on contraception depending upon whether the views of atheists are in accordance with Christian teaching or their personal beliefs.

Activities ?

1 Discuss with a partner what you think about the different Christian attitudes towards contraception. Give reasons for and against your statements.

2 Summarise three different attitudes towards contraception using a table to present your work.

3 Imagine you work for an aid agency either in Africa, where there is an AIDS epidemic, or in Latin America where there is the Zika virus. Write a letter to the Pope explaining why some people think that the Roman Catholic teachings on contraception should change.

Extend your knowledge

- Humanae Vitae 14 says contraception is 'any action which, either in anticipation of the conjugal act [sexual intercourse], or in its accomplishment, or in the development of its natural consequences, proposes, whether as an end or as a means, to render procreation impossible'. In other words, all artificial contraception is wrong.
- Roman Catholics can only use Natural Family Planning (NFP). NFP is based on the time women are least likely to conceive. The Roman Catholic Church teaches that this is morally acceptable. Many people criticise this method, as it relies on a woman's menstrual cycle being regular, which is often not the case.

Exam-style question

Explain two different attitudes towards family planning and the regulation of births. You must refer to a source of wisdom and authority in your answer. **(5 marks)**

Exam tip

Ensure you can compare and contrast different Christian teachings and attitudes towards family planning and the regulation of births. Make sure that you refer to Humanae Vitae as a source of wisdom and authority for Roman Catholic teaching.

Summary

- Christian Churches have different teachings about contraception.
- The attitudes of Christians towards family planning and the regulation of births vary between denominations and within the same Church.
- The Church of England and other protestant traditions like the Methodist Church agree with the responsible use of contraception.
- The Roman Catholic Church gives its view on contraception in a document called Humanae Vitae.
- The Roman Catholic Church disagrees with all artificial methods of contraception, but permits a natural method based on a woman's menstrual cycle.
- Some Roman Catholics think artificial methods are more practical in the modern world.
- Humanists are very supportive of the use of contraception providing the outcomes are positive.

Checkpoint

Strengthen

S1 How does the Church of England teaching on contraception, family planning and the regulation of births compare to the Roman Catholic teaching on these matters?

S2 What reasons does the Methodist Church give for allowing contraception?

S3 Why do Humanists believe that contraception is not a moral or ethical issue?

Challenge

C1 Why might the spread of AIDS in Africa and emergence of the Zika virus in Latin America challenge Roman Catholic teaching on contraception?

C2 What moral issues are connected with the use of contraception?

C3 Why do you think Humanists have been keen to promote the use of contraception?

3.6 Divorce

Learning objectives

- To understand different Christian teachings and attitudes towards divorce and remarriage.
- To understand Humanist and atheist attitudes towards divorce and remarriage.

Biblical teaching on divorce

Biblical teaching on divorce is unclear. In ancient times only men could say they wanted a divorce, sometimes for very minor reasons. Remarriage after divorce was permitted, but not for everyone. For example, a husband and wife could not remarry each other if:

- they divorced, then
- the wife married someone else and became divorced again.

Sources of authority

If a man marries a woman [then] writes her a certificate of divorce [he] is not allowed to marry her again [if she has been spoiled] (Deuteronomy 24:1–4).

This is because the wife would be seen as 'spoiled'.

In one part of the New Testament Jesus suggests that:

- a man can only divorce his wife if she commits 'sexual immorality', **commits adultery**
- a divorced woman is a 'victim of adultery'
- a man who marries a divorced woman commits adultery
- therefore, remarriage after divorce is not allowed.

In other places, the New Testament is not clear whether *divorce* is forbidden or *remarriage after divorce* is forbidden.

Another passage says that, in cases like desertion, divorce is allowed. Here's an example:

- either the husband or the wife is a non-believer (non-Christian), then
- the non-believer leaves the marriage (deserter), this means
- the partner who remains can remarry.

Sources of authority

When Jesus had finished saying these things, he left Galilee and went into the region of Judea to the other side of the Jordan. Large crowds followed him, and he healed them there.

Some Pharisees came to him to test him. They asked, "Is it lawful for a man to divorce his wife for any and every reason?"

"Haven't you read," he replied, "that at the beginning the Creator 'made them male and female,' and said, 'For this reason a man will leave his father and mother and be united to his wife, and the two will become one flesh'? So they are no longer two, but one flesh. Therefore what God has joined together, let no one separate."

"Why then," they asked, "did Moses command that a man give his wife a certificate of divorce and send her away?"

Jesus replied, "Moses permitted you to divorce your wives because your hearts were hard. But it was not this way from the beginning. I tell you that anyone who divorces his wife, except for sexual immorality, and marries another woman commits adultery."

The disciples said to him, "If this is the situation between a husband and wife, it is better not to marry."

Jesus replied, "Not everyone can accept this word, but only those to whom it has been given. For there are eunuchs who were born that way, and there are eunuchs who have been made eunuchs by others— and there are those who choose to live like eunuchs for the sake of the kingdom of heaven. The one who can accept this should accept it." (Matthew 19:1–12)

Sources of authority

[If a man] has a wife who is not a believer and she is willing to live with him, he must not divorce her. And if a woman has a husband who is not a believer and he is willing to live with her, she must not divorce him. But if the unbeliever leaves, let it be so … [The partner remaining] is not bound in such circumstances (1 Corinthians 7:12–15).

Christian teaching and attitudes towards divorce

Christian Churches differ in their teaching about divorce and remarriage. Christianity teaches that marriage is a lifelong relationship.

During the Christian marriage ceremony couples promise to stay together for the rest of their lives. However, many Christian Churches accept that life does not always work out as planned.

They recognise that, sadly, things can go wrong and marriages break down for many reasons.

Nevertheless, these Christian Churches still, Christian Churches encourage couples to do whatever they can to repair their marriage (including marriage counselling) before getting a divorce.

Some Christians believe that while marriage is very important:

- humans do make mistakes, and
- God is omnibenevolent, all loving, and would not want those involved (including children) to suffer because of an unhappy or failing marriage.

Christians who support divorce may also think that sometimes it is too easy to get one.

Situation ethics

Christian attitudes towards divorce can be influenced by a philosophical idea known as **situation ethics**. This is where the circumstances of each individual situation are considered very carefully and Christians make a decision about whether something is morally right or wrong based on the principle of agape and what the most loving thing to do is for everyone involved.

What the Roman Catholic Church teaches about divorce

The Roman Catholic Church:

- is against divorce
- forbids divorced people to remarry
- teaches that marriage is a spiritual bond that is permanent and binding. This bond cannot be broken on Earth as human laws cannot separate what God has joined together.

Sources of authority

Therefore what God has joined together, let no one separate (Mark 10:9).

Extend your knowledge

In July 2002, the General Synod (the Church of England's highest authority) said:

- '[Marriage] should always be undertaken as a solemn, public and life-long covenant between a man and a woman'.
- '[But] some marriages… fail and the Church's care for couples in that situation should be of paramount importance.'
- 'There are exceptional circumstances in which a divorced person may be married in church during the lifetime of a former spouse.' (This would depend on the **clergy**, formal religious leader within some religions, the parish priest or the Christian **minister**, a member of the clergy in some churches, who would marry them.)

Sources of authority

'Marriage is created by God to be a lifelong relationship between a man and woman. The church expects all couples seeking marriage to intend to live together "for better for worse… till death us do part". It is not, then, a light matter to solemnise a marriage in which one partner has a previous partner still living. It is important that the decision you take as to whether to solemnise such a marriage should be on the basis of clear principles that are consistent with the church's teaching.' (Advice to clergy from the General Synod.)

Some Roman Catholics with broken marriages choose to live apart rather than divorce. This is because they do not want to go against the teachings of their Church. The Roman Catholic Church accepts that, in some cases, a Catholic can be divorced. For example:

- if there was domestic violence in the marriage
- if the husband or wife did not want to get divorced, but their partner gave them no choice.

Sources of authority

'We know the sadness of those who do not have access to sacramental communion because of their family situations that do not conform to the commandment of the Lord. Some divorced and remarried people sadly accept their inability to take sacramental communion and they make an offering of it to God. Others are not able to understand this restriction, and live with an internal frustration. We reaffirm that, while we do not endorse their choice, they are not excluded from the life of the Church. We ask that they participate in Sunday Mass and devote themselves assiduously to listening to the Word of God so that it might nourish their life of faith, of love and of conversion. We wish to tell them how close we are to them in prayer and pastoral concern. Together, let us ask the Lord to obey his will faithfully.' (General Synod of Catholic Bishops, 2005)

Roman Catholics who have divorced and remarried are seen by the Catholic Church to have committed a grave sin. They are not allowed to take part in the Eucharist, but they can still attend church. There is an exception to this: if the marriage has been annulled. An **annulment** is a declaration from the Roman Catholic Church that the marriage was never valid in the first place, for example, if someone was:

- forced to marry against their will, or
- psychologically unable to understand what the commitment of marriage meant.

What Humanists and atheists think about divorce

Humanists think that marriage breakdowns can cause problems, particularly for children. They think:

- it is better for two parents to share the work and pleasure of bringing up children
- husbands and wives should be realistic about marriage (for example, it's not always romantic)
- sometimes divorce is the best option because it ends conflict
- if divorce is handled well, it could improve the quality of life for those involved.

Humanists do not believe that marriage is a sacred institution because they do not believe in God. They support:

- personal freedom
- liberal divorce laws
- the ability to remarry.

In the USA, research suggests that atheists have lower divorce rates than some groups of Christians. An atheist might argue this is because their relationship does not focus on a supernatural power, which means the couple have more time for each other. However, this does not mean that atheists are either for or against divorce and remarriage.

Can you remember?

- What do some people say is the biggest challenge for Christian parents?
- How might local churches support families?
- Why might the support of the local church be important to Christian families?

Exam-style question

Explain two reasons why Christians might either agree or disagree with divorce.

You must refer to a source of wisdom and authority in your answer. **(5 marks)**

Activities

1 List the different Christian arguments for and against divorce and remarriage.
2 With a partner, role-play a Christian and a Humanist discussing their beliefs about marriage and divorce.
3 Discuss in groups why you think divorce rates have increased over the last 100 years.

Exam tip

Make sure that you know and can explain different Christian teachings and attitudes towards divorce and remarriage.

Summary

- Biblical teaching on divorce and remarriage is inconsistent.
- Different Christian Churches have different teachings and attitudes towards divorce and remarriage.
- All Christians agree that, ideally, marriages should last a lifetime.
- Some Christian Churches, like the Church of England, accept that sometimes divorce is the 'most loving thing to do' for all concerned.
- Churches that accept divorce will also in exceptional circumstances permit remarriage in a church.
- The Roman Catholic Church does not permit divorce. It will not let Catholics who have remarried without an annulment take part in the Eucharist.
- Humanist views on divorce sometimes agree with Christian views.
- However, Humanists do not believe that marriage is a sacred relationship. They also support easier divorce laws, which many Christians might disagree with.

Checkpoint

Strengthen

S1 Why might some Christians disagree with divorce and remarriage?

S2 How has the Bible helped to influence Christian teachings on divorce and remarriage?

S3 How do Humanist and Christian attitudes towards divorce and remarriage compare?

Challenge

C1 How can situation ethics be applied to divorce and remarriage?

C2 Why do you think a remarried Roman Catholic might feel frustrated that they cannot take part in the Eucharist?

C3 What reassurances do you think a Christian priest might need before agreeing to remarry a divorced person?

3.7 Equality of men and women in the family

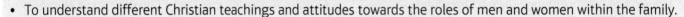

Learning objectives

- To understand different Christian teachings and attitudes towards the roles of men and women within the family.
- To understand different atheist and Humanist attitudes towards the roles of men and women within the family.

What Christians think about equality in the family

Christian attitudes towards the roles of men and women within the family vary.

Some Christians believe the roles of men and women should follow Genesis 2:18, Ephesians 5:21–30 and 1 Peter 3:1–7. The literal interpretation of the translation of these biblical texts has helped to form a traditional model of the family, which is **patriarchal**, meaning:

- the husband is the head of the household
- the wife obeys and supports her husband (which includes looking after the children and running a Christian home)
- men must love and respect their wives (as they love themselves), and be considerate
- women are thought of as the weaker partner in the marriage
- women are also thought of as mothers.

Sources of authority

The Lord God said, 'It is not good for the man to be alone. I will make a helper suitable for him' (Genesis 2:18).

These days, many Christians believe that the traditional family model is not in keeping with modern life and society. Whereas the Roman Catholic Church maintaines that:

- the Church, and its followers, must be true to the authority of the Bible; it is the word of God and cannot change its views to fit in with the latest ideas
- men and women were both created in God's image (Genesis 1:27) but were given different roles
- Adam, who represents all men, was created to work and look after the Garden of Eden (Genesis 2:15)
- Eve, who represents all women, was designed to help Adam with this (Genesis 2:18)

Sources of authority

Wives, submit yourselves to your own husbands as you do to the Lord. For the husband is the head of the wife as Christ is the head of the church, his body, of which he is the Saviour. Now as the church submits to Christ, so also wives should submit to their husbands in everything. Husbands, love your wives, just as Christ loved the church and gave himself up for her to make her holy, cleansing her by the washing with water through the word, and to present her to himself as a radiant church, without stain or wrinkle or any other blemish, but holy and blameless. In this same way, husbands ought to love their wives as their own bodies. He who loves his wife loves himself. After all, no one ever hated their own body, but they feed and care for their body, just as Christ does the church – for we are members of his body (Ephesians 5:22–30).

Wives, in the same way submit yourselves to your own husbands so that, if any of them do not believe the word, they may be won over without words by the behaviour of their wives, when they see the purity and reverence of your lives. Your beauty should not come from outward adornment, such as elaborate hairstyles and the wearing of gold jewellery or fine clothes. Rather, it should be that of your inner self, the unfading beauty of a gentle and quiet spirit, which is of great worth in God's sight. For this is the way the holy women of the past who put their hope in God used to adorn themselves. They submitted themselves to their own husbands, like Sarah, who obeyed Abraham and called him her lord. You are her daughters if you do what is right and do not give way to fear. Husbands, in the same way be considerate as you live with your wives, and treat them with respect as the weaker partner and as heirs with you of the gracious gift of life, so that nothing will hinder your prayers (1 Peter 3:1–7).

- God's intention therefore was for men and women to be seen as equal but with different roles.

For the Roman Catholic Church this view extends into Church leadership; this means women are not allowed to become priests.

Some Christians disagree with this. They think that if men and women were created in 'the image of God' there is no real difference between them. This means that the roles of men and women within the family:

- do not need to follow the traditional patriarchal model
- can be flexible according to the wishes and needs of couples today.

For example:

- a wife might be the higher wage earner and the husband might stay at home to look after the children, or
- a couple might both work, share the household chores and responsibility for running the home.

Christians might refer to Galatians 3:28 to support their arguments.

The Church of England and many other Protestant Churches accept that men and women are equal in all areas of life, including church leadership.

Sources of authority

There is neither Jew nor Gentile, neither slave nor free, nor is there male and female, for you are all one in Christ Jesus (Galatians 3:28).

What atheists and Humanists think about equality in the family

Many atheists, particularly **feminist** atheists, criticise traditional Christian teaching on the family roles of men and women. They say traditional, biblical models (for example, as taught by the Roman Catholic Church) have been responsible for the mistreatment, repression and inequality of women throughout the world for centuries.

The British Humanist Association thinks the traditional model of family roles described on page ?? is not very common these days. They welcome a range of family roles and say:

- people must have roles that work for them
- everyone should be happy with the role they have been given/chosen
- men and women are equal
- family roles should not be based on gender alone (for example, a woman looks after children while a man goes to work).

Figure 3.6 Christian stereotypes of family roles

'I have endeavored to dissipate these religious superstitions from the minds of women, and base their faith on science and reason, where I found myself at last that peace and comfort I could never find in the Bible and the church... The less they believe, the better for their own happiness and development...

The Bible and the Church have been the greatest stumbling blocks in the way of women's emancipation.'.

Figure 3.7 The words of Elizabeth Cady Stanton, 19th-century atheist and early leader of the women's rights movement

Exam-style question

Explain two different Christian attitudes towards the family roles of men and women.

You must refer to a source of wisdom and authority in your answer. **(5 marks)**

Exam tip

Make sure you can describe a range of different Christian and non-Christian views about the roles of men and women within the family.

Activities

1 Explain how biblical teachings about family roles are reflected in the image of a Christian family stereotype.
2 With a partner, identify and describe a variety of modern family roles for men and women that might be more representative of families today rather than the traditional Christian model of family roles.
3 In groups, find a summary of the book called *Does God Hate Women?* Discuss why Christians might agree or disagree with the themes it covers.

Extend your knowledge

Christian Feminism is a Christian movement that explores and promotes the equality of men and women within society and the Christian faith. Christian feminists:

- are particularly interested in Church leadership (the ordination of women) and marital roles within a Christian marriage
- believe women have been disadvantaged because of how they have been represented in Christianity
- argue for equal recognition of women's moral and spiritual abilities
- argue for choices around having children
- think the feminine or gender-transcendent qualities within God should be acknowledged
- say that God should not be presumed/referred to as male. Some people might take this to mean 'because God is male, male is God'. Christian feminists believe this attitude has resulted in unfair gender inequalities.

Summary

- There are different teachings and attitudes towards the family roles of men and women within Christianity.
- The Roman Catholic Church teaching is based on a traditional biblical model. It states that men and women have been created equal by God but for different purposes.
- This means that the roles of men and women within the family are defined according to the Bible.
- Many Christians disagree with this. They believe this view is no longer suitable for modern society.
- The Church of England and many other Protestant Churches support flexible gender roles within the family, depending on the needs of the family. Both sides of this debate use biblical texts to support their views.
- Humanists believe that men and women should both be happy with the roles they play within the family.
- Some atheists, particularly feminist atheists, are very critical of the traditional Christian family roles for men and women. They say these beliefs have caused the mistreatment of women within the family and society.

Checkpoint

Strengthen

S1 What does Christianity teach about the roles of men and women within the family?
S2 How has the Bible influenced Christian attitudes towards gender roles?
S3 Why might the traditional Christian model of the role of men and women within the family be criticised by atheists and Humanists?

Challenge

C1 Why do you think a Christian might refer to Galatians 3:28 to support their argument for a more egalitarian model of family roles?
C2 Explain why religious stereotypes might be unhelpful to an understanding of family roles.
C3 Why might an atheist like Elizabeth Cady Stanton say that 'the Bible and the Church have been the greatest stumbling blocks in women's emancipation'?

3.8 Gender prejudice and discrimination

Learning objectives

- To understand the meaning of gender prejudice and discrimination.
- To understand how Christians have opposed gender prejudice and discrimination.
- To understand atheist and Humanist attitudes towards gender prejudice and discrimination.

The meaning of gender prejudice and discrimination

The term **prejudice** means to pre-judge someone based on a fixed idea or belief that generally is not true. Prejudice is often linked to the idea of stereotyping. A **stereotype** assumes that people from the same group (for example, religion, race, social, gender, etc.) behave in the same way.

Discrimination is what happens when an individual or group is treated differently because of others' prejudices about them. There are two types of discrimination: negative and positive.

- Negative discrimination relates to people or groups who are disadvantaged because, for no good reason, they don't have the same opportunities and rights as others.

- Positive discrimination relates to people or groups who are treated more favourably for what are believed to be good reasons. An example might be top universities offering individuals from disadvantaged backgrounds more places than individuals from privileged backgrounds.

The practice of positive discrimination can be very controversial. Some people argue very strongly against it. They say that university places or jobs, for example, should be given just on merit. Gender prejudice and discrimination happens when assumptions are made about individuals or groups because of their gender and are treated differently because of it. Another term for gender prejudice and discrimination is '**sexism/sexist**'. Someone who discriminates against someone on the basis of gender can be regarded as 'sexist'.

Christian opposition to gender prejudice and discrimination

Many Christians and non-Christians would argue that the Christian Church has much to answer for regarding gender prejudice and discrimination even though some

verses in the Bible, such as Galatians 3:28, support gender equality. The issue of sexism and women in the Christian Church has been widely discussed. Two key areas for debate are the role of women within the family and whether women can become priests and bishops (see Topic 2.7). For example, in the Roman Catholic Church, women are not allowed to become priests or bishops, whereas in the Church of England and other Protestant Churches they can become a member of the clergy. Similarly, the Roman Catholic Church teaches that women within the family should fulfil a traditional role. Some other Christian churches like the Church of England disagree with this and say that a more **egalitarian** model of family life is preferable in modern times.

Figure 3.8 The Church League for Women's Suffrage was founded by the Reverend Claude Hinscliffe and his wife Gertrude. They campaigned to secure parliamentary voting rights for women but also hoped to draw attention to the 'deep religious significance of the movement'

Figure 3.9 A Christian action group campaigns for women priests in the Catholic Church

Sources of authority

Before the coming of this faith, we were held in custody under the law, locked up until the faith that was to come would be revealed. So the law was our guardian until Christ came that we might be justified by faith. Now that this faith has come, we are no longer under a guardian. So in Christ Jesus you are all children of God through faith, for all of you who were baptized into Christ have clothed yourselves with Christ. There is neither Jew nor Gentile, neither slave nor free, nor is there male and female, for you are all one in Christ Jesus. If you belong to Christ, then you are Abraham's seed, and heirs according to the promise. (Galatians 3:23–29)

Christian Aid

Christian Aid is an international Christian charity that works with people of all religions and those without a belief in God in more than 50 countries throughout the world. Achieving gender equality lies at the heart of Christian Aid's work. It believes that:

- the main causes of poverty are the unequal distribution of power, and the unfair abuses of power
- the greatest and most widespread unequal distribution of power and the most unfair abuses of power are between men and women.

Extend your knowledge

'We cannot stamp out poverty without addressing the fundamental inequality between the sexes… The discrimination or subordination of one gender by another is a global issue… it undermines our own theological understandings that all people are of equal and unique value and worth… Gender is a universal power relationship – shaping men's and women's choices and opportunities in every sphere (political, economic, social, interpersonal) and at every level from household to global. While other structures (such as ethnicity, age, disability, caste, sexuality) can have a more profound impact on individuals, gender is all-pervasive – we're all gendered, and we all act every day within and upon a web of gender relationships. Every one of us is personally implicated in gender as a question of power. However, although we're all part of the problem, we're also all part of the solution.' (Christian Aid)

Christian Aid believes that gender inequality:
- is wrong
- goes against Christian beliefs of equality
- is contrary to the Universal Declaration of Human Rights
- will impact particularly on women from birth to death; this is because in many societies boys are considered more important than girls, which can lead to the deliberate killing of baby girls (selective gender infanticide).

However, Christian Aid accepts that gender inequality makes it hard:
- to be a daughter, mother or wife in today's society
- for men to play the traditional roles expected of them.

This is why it works to achieve economic, environmental, political and social justice in partnership with:
- girls and boys, men and women, families
- communities
- Churches and faith groups
- governments.

The Christian Aid vision of gender equality is men and women 'living lives of dignity free from fear and oppression… men and women live alongside one another in peaceful and just relationships, equal in God's sight.'

Many Churches and individual Christians from all denominations support the work of Christian Aid. There is an annual Christian Aid week in the UK, which draws attention to its work and helps to raise funds for its campaigns.

Figure 3.10 Tearfund is an international Christian charity that works with people of all faiths

Tearfund

Tearfund is another international Christian charity that works with religious and non-religious people – worldwide. It also:

- campaigns for gender equality
- makes sure its work is sensitive to gender
- recognises the equal worth of men and women.

Tearfund says that *'Global poverty has a woman's face'*. It encourages churches across the world to:

- help eradicate gender prejudice and discrimination
- support and encourage gender equality.

Just like Christian Aid, Tearfund's work is inspired by Christian beliefs about:

- stewardship
- the responsibilities Christians have towards others
- the example set by Jesus.

Tearfund's work on gender has led to the establishment of 'Restored'. Restored is an international Christian Alliance that draws churches' attention to violence against women both inside and outside of church communities.

Sources of authority

'Jesus treated both men and women as individuals, worthy of his full attention. He encouraged and affirmed women throughout his teaching, at a time when society gave women little value.' (Tearfund)

Atheist and Humanist attitudes towards gender prejudice

There are many more male than female atheists. This could be because women are seen as more religious than men. However, there has always been a strong feminist tradition within atheism that has focused on gender discrimination and inequality. Historically, the fight for women's rights has often criticised religions like Christianity that are seen as patriarchal.

Activities

1 Explain what the terms discrimination, gender, prejudice, stereotype and sexism mean.
2 With a partner, identify some gender stereotypes and come up with examples that disprove them.
3 Discuss in groups why Christians might argue that the suffrage movement had a 'deep religious significance'?

Exam-style question

'Feminism is anti-religion.'
Evaluate this statement considering arguments for and against.
In your response you should:
• refer to Christian teachings
• refer to different Christian points of view
• reach a justified conclusion.
(12 marks)

Exam tip

Make sure you know the work being done by individual Christians, Christian churches and Christian organisations to address gender prejudice and discrimination.

Summary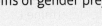

• Prejudice and discrimination happens when people are pre-judged; this can lead to stereotyping.
• Gender prejudice and discrimination happens when individuals or groups are treated differently because of what is believed about a particular gender. This is also known as sexism.
• Both males and females can be affected by gender prejudice and discrimination.
• Historically, and in the present day, women have been disadvantaged in many ways as a result of gender prejudice (also men but to a lesser degree).
• Christianity has been criticised for its attitudes towards women.
• Some people still believe that sexism exists in some parts of the Christian Church, particularly with regard to leadership opportunities for women.
• Many individual Christians, Christian Churches and Christian organisations oppose gender prejudice and discrimination.
• Humanists oppose gender prejudice and discrimination.
• The rights of women are an important concern for some other atheists.

Checkpoint

Strengthen

S1 Why can prejudice lead to stereotyping and discrimination?
S2 How are some women disadvantaged in today's world?
S3 What have Christians done to oppose gender prejudice and discrimination?

Challenge

C1 Why might some people say that the Christian Church has 'much to answer for' in terms of gender prejudice and discrimination?
C2 What reasons might there be for women being more religious than men?
C3 Why do you think Christian Aid says 'we're all part of the problem, we're also all part of the solution' for issues of gender inequality?

Recap: Marriage and the family

Use the activities and exam-style questions on the following pages to reinforce your learning before you move on to the next chapter.

Recall quiz

Marriage

1   What role does the Bible play in developing Christian beliefs about marriage, sexual relationships, divorce, the family and gender roles?

2   What do Christians believe about the importance and purpose of marriage?

Sexual relationships

3   What attitudes do Christians have towards sexual relationships?

4   Why might some Christians disagree with contraception and family planning?

Families

5   What do Christians believe to be the purpose of the family?

Support for families in the local parish

6   How might the local parish support families?

Divorce

7   What do Christians think about divorce and remarriage?

Gender prejudice and discrimination

8   Why might Christians oppose gender prejudice and discrimination?

9   What do Humanists and atheists believe with regard to marriage, sexual relationships, divorce, the family and gender prejudice and discrimination?

Activities ?

1   Produce a glossary of all the key terms in this chapter.

2   Design a leaflet showing how a local church could support families.

3   Role-play in groups an atheist, a Humanist and two Christians with different attitudes discussing contraception.

4   Use the information in the Summary for each topic in this chapter to prepare revision materials. This could take the form of revision cards for each topic in this chapter or a concept map that notes the key ideas and learning points. Remember to:

   • use and highlight the key terms, making sure that you know what they mean

   • include relevant biblical references.

5   Discuss with a partner why some Christians might use situation ethics to help determine their attitude towards divorce.

Exam-style questions

a Explain two circumstances under which a Roman Catholic marriage might be annulled. **(4 marks)**

b Outline three reasons why the family is important to Christians. **(3 marks)**

c Explain two different Christian attitudes towards either sexual relationships outside of marriage or homosexuality.

You must refer to a source of wisdom and authority. **(5 marks)**

In this question, 3 of the marks awarded will be for your spelling, punctuation and grammar and your use of specialist terminology.

d 'Contraception leads to sexual immorality.'

Evaluate this statement considering arguments for and against. In your response you should:

- refer to Christian teachings
- refer to non-religious points of view
- reach a justified conclusion. **(15 marks)**

Exam tips

a Make sure you can explain the difference between a divorce and annulment.

b Make sure you can explain the importance and purpose of family from a Christian and other perspectives.

c Ensure that you know Christian teachings and different Christian attitudes towards sexual relationships and homosexuality.

d Make sure you can explain, giving examples to support your statements, a range of views about the use of contraception, including at least two different Christian responses supported by sources of authority.

Summary of learning

You have learned what Christianity teaches and what Christians believe about:

- the importance and purpose of marriage
- the right relationship for sexual relationships and having children
- the importance and purpose of the family, and the various types of families in modern life
- the responsibility they have to the family, and the role of the Church to provide support and care
- the use of contraception, both historically and in families today
- divorce and remarriage, and the inconsistencies of Biblical teachings
- how men and women should ideally behave within the family
- prejudice, discrimination, sexism and stereotyping, and how to overcome these things.

You have also learned about Humanist and atheist attitudes towards these issues.

Extend: Marriage and the family

Christians would argue that getting married in a church is very important. The Church of England has written some material to explain why Christians believe this. Reading the articles and doing the activities below, together with the other things you have learned in this chapter, will help you to answer the exam question at the end of this section.

Source 1

Why get married in a church?

Churches are special places and there are some things about a church wedding that you just can't get anywhere else.

A church is so much more than simply a venue for your wedding. Unique and special things become part of your marriage, on the day itself and beyond.

A church wedding will add a spiritual dimension to your marriage. The ceremony includes God and looks to him for help and guidance. God's blessing is the main attraction for many couples, whatever their beliefs.

You can make amazing vows, or promises, in a church. You can only make vows this big in a church. These vows, made in public, will help you to stay together and grow together. God and your church are there for you to help you keep your vows.

The Vicar has a very particular role to play in your wedding. They can blend ancient tradition and modern experience to reflect your story. Because of the relationship with the Vicar, your wedding can be made personal, memorable, meaningful and beautiful.

Church buildings offer outstanding beauty. Old or new, intimate or grand, our 16,000 churches are some of the nation's most stunning wedding venues, with two-thirds being listed buildings.

Church buildings offer centuries of history. Imagine all the couples who have married in your local church, some of whom may well be your family. You can feel you're becoming part of history itself, the bigger plan, by marrying in the same place as your relatives. We know these sorts of connections can make your day even more special.

You can be involved in making choices about your ceremony. You can even use our online ceremony planner to get you started.

For some people, a church simply seems like the proper place to get married. Churches can be described as 'peaceful', 'serene', or having an atmosphere that makes marrying there a particularly special experience.

And after your wedding, you'll realise that a church is more than simply a wedding venue. We'll always be here for you: http://www. yourchurchwedding.org/article/more-than-a-wedding-venue/

(The Church of England)

Exam tips

- Learn to spell the common words you might need to use in your answers – for example, *annulment, atheist, believe, beliefs, Humanist, Christians, Christianity, discrimination, marriage, patriarch, prejudice, sexism*.

- Use capital letters for the beginning of sentences and nouns (names of things). In Christianity, always use capitals for *God, Trinity, Holy Spirit, Jesus and Bible*. Always use capitals for different denominations or churches – for example, the *Church of England*, the *Roman Catholic Church*.

- Use apostrophes correctly – for example, *Jesus' teachings*. Note, the *teachings of Jesus* does not need an apostrophe.

- Use a good range of specialist terms (check the Glossary).

- Use paragraphs to separate different ideas, points or opinions.

- Use a full stop to mark the end of every sentence. Do not make your sentences too long!

- Read through what you have written to check it is clear, makes sense and has answered the question. Do not waffle or rant. Instead, write in a calm and measured way.

Activities ?

1 Read Source 1 on your own, with a partner or in a group. Then answer the questions below.

   a Why might people say that church buildings are special?

   b What words might a Christian use to describe the atmosphere in church?

   c In what ways is a vicar or priest different from a **registrar**, someone legally able to conduct civil wedding ceremonies?

   d What role does a vicar or priest play during the wedding ceremony? (Also think about who or what the vicar/priest represents.)

   e Why do you think Christians say that you can only make vows this big in Church?

   f What do you think the statement 'a church is more than simply a wedding venue' means?

   g In what ways could the Church support a couple after they are married?

   h Why might some people say you should only get married in church if you are a Christian?

   i What do you think the Church of England's article is trying to achieve and how could this be linked to evangelism?

2 A Christian marriage ceremony, like other religious ceremonies, has lots of religious symbolism. Look at Source 2, on page 105, taken during a Christian wedding service. Write down what you think is happening at this point in the service. Identify the things you see in the image that you think are symbolic, explaining why.

3 Look up the legal forms of words that can be used during a marriage ceremony. How do they differ? Write down any differences, then explain which version you prefer and why. Give reasons for your answers and draw on the Christian teachings to support or disagree with those reasons.

Source 2

The Church of England has three legal forms of words that can be used during a marriage ceremony. The most modern version is from 2000

Exam-style question

In this question 3 of the marks awarded will be for your spelling, punctuation and grammar and your use of specialist terminology.

'Marriage is the perfect state.'

Evaluate this statement considering arguments for and against. In your answer you should refer to:

– Christian teachings

– reach a justified conclusion.

(15 marks)

Exam tip

Before you answer a question, think about *everything* you have learned about the topic before you start to write. Avoid rushing an answer with what first comes to mind. Some of the longer answer questions are deliberately written in a way that might cause you to answer in a one-sided way!

4 Matters of life and death

Matters of life and death are things to do with the beginning and the end of life. Very often matters of life and death raise moral issues and give rise to ultimate questions. An ultimate question is a very important question to which there is thought to be no definite or absolute answer. Some examples of ultimate questions are:

- Where does life come from?
- Why do we exist?
- When does life begin?
- What is the purpose of life?
- What happens when we die?

Morality is about right and wrong behaviour. A **moral** issue is something that might be considered right or wrong for a variety of reasons, such as the laws of a country, the teachings of a religion or the beliefs and values of an individual or community. A moral decision is where a choice needs to be made between what is considered the right thing or the wrong thing to do. Not all the decisions people have to make are moral decisions.

The word **immoral** means something that is not morally right and can be understood in various ways such as bad, wrongful, unethical, unfair. The word **amoral** means 'without moral standards or principles'. A person who acts in an amoral way is unconcerned with what is right or wrong from a moral perspective.

People have different moral codes and personal **values**, which they live their lives by depending upon their culture, background and personal experiences. Values are the things that people think are important in life, such as honesty, trust, truth, hard work or a respect for life, family, authority, etc. A person's core values provide a framework within which they make moral decisions. A Christian's values, like other people who are religious, are shaped by their faith. The term Christian values, historically, refers to the values that come from the teachings of Jesus as set out in the Bible.

Christians try to live their lives in the way they think God wants. They believe that one of the reasons God sent Jesus to Earth was to show human beings the right way to live. When making a moral decision, many Christians would ask 'What would Jesus do in this situation?'. They would then try to follow his example. Jesus' life and teachings are one of the main sources of moral authority for Christians.

Christians can find out what Jesus might have done by reading the Gospels in the Bible. The Bible also contains other teachings about the right way to live, together with religious laws such as the words of the **prophets** and the Ten Commandments. In some situations, the Bible can only act as a guide and Christians may turn to other sources of authority to help them make a decision.

In this chapter you will find out what Christians believe about:

- scientific explanations for the origins of the universe and the value of the universe
- the sanctity of life
- non-religious explanations for the origins and value of human life
- abortion
- death and the afterlife
- euthanasia
- the natural world.

Checkpoint

Recall

Before starting this chapter, you should remember the following.

- Matters of life and death are to do with the beginning and end of life.
- There can often be moral issues associated with the beginning and end of life. A moral issue is something that is right or wrong.
- Matters of life and death can also raise ultimate questions. An ultimate question is one to which there is no definite or absolute answer.
- People have different moral codes and personal values depending upon their background and experiences.
- Traditionally, Christian values are based on the teachings of Jesus as set out in the Bible.
- The Bible is a source of moral authority for Christians. A source of moral authority is something that tells you what to do or guides you. Other sources of moral authority for Christians are the teachings of their Church and the advice of other Christians, particularly their priest or vicar. A Christian might also pray for guidance and listen to what their conscience is telling them to do.
- Christians always try to live their life in the way they think God wants them to.

Look ahead

Following this chapter, you will prepare for your Christianity Paper 1 exam.

4.1 The origins and value of the universe

Cosmology

Many people think that the question of how the universe came into being is one of the biggest mysteries in life. Some people might say that it is the greatest mystery of all time because so many other ultimate questions are linked to it.

Cosmology is 'the science of the study of the origins of the universe and its development'. The word cosmology comes from two Greek word *kosmos* meaning 'world' and *logia* meaning 'study of'. In modern cosmology, the **Big Bang theory** is the main idea which has been put forward to explain how the universe came into existence.

The ideas that underpin the Big Bang theory were developed by a Roman Catholic priest and scientist called Georges Lemaitre (1894–1966). Lemaitre was an astronomer and professor of Physics at a Catholic university in Belgium. He is credited with two key ideas, which have had a big impact on the way that science understands the beginning and the development of the universe. The first theory Lemaitre put forward in 1927 was the **Theory of the Expanding Universe**. This is the hypothesis that the universe has been expanding outwards and possibly into infinity, ever since it came into being. The **universe** is a term used to describe everything that exists from the smallest atom to the largest galaxy, a collection of stars, gas and dust held together by gravity. According to physicists, there are at least one hundred billion observable galaxies in the universe. The Earth sits in a galaxy known as the Milky Way.

Lemaitre built upon his Theory of the Expanding Universe and developed the idea that the expansion of the universe could be traced back in time to a single point of origin. He suggested that the universe itself emerged from an extremely small, very dense and tremendously hot state, known as the Singularity. He referred to this idea as a hypothesis of the 'primeval atom' or the 'Cosmic Egg', which was later to become known as the Big Bang theory. Today, the Big Bang theory is the main argument put forward to explain the beginning of the universe, although not all cosmologists, people who study the origins of the universe, agree with this.

Figure 4.1 The Messier 81 (M81) galaxy is located about 12 million light-years away in the Ursa Major constellation, M81 is among the brightest of the galaxies visible by telescope from Earth

Christian responses to the work of Georges Lemaitre

Lemaitre was deeply religious and it might seem reasonable to assume that his Christian beliefs led him to the idea of creation beginning at a point in time, as the Bible suggests in Genesis 1–2. However, he always insisted that this was not the case and totally discouraged anyone from referring to or connecting the 'primeval atom' with the act of Creation by God. Lemaitre said that his work as a scientist was not influenced by his Christian faith. He stated that science is concerned with truth and is impartial to religion. Equally, he maintained that God did not need science to prove divine creation and that God could not be reduced to a scientific theory as the activities of God remain hidden.

Figure 4.2 Georges Lemaitre

Sometimes science and religion can seem to be in conflict with each other, as scientific theories and religious arguments may seek to prove different points. Lemaitre taught that there need not be conflict between religious and scientific views about the origins of the universe. However, this was not because Lemaitre thought that scientific views could explain or support religious beliefs but because he thought that the presence of God in Creation is above and beyond scientific explanation. Many Christians agree with this. Other Christians say that 'good Science is good theology'; and they look to scientific theories like the Big Bang theory, the Theory of the Expanding Universe and the Theory of Evolution to explain how God created and developed the universe. Creationists do not accept any scientific explanations connected with the origins or development of the universe.

John Polkinghorne, a former Professor of Mathematical Physics at Cambridge University and an Anglican Priest, has a different view. He believes that science and religion can have a much closer relationship since they both look for truth but they ask different questions. Science poses questions like 'What?', 'When?', 'Where?', and 'How?', whereas religion is interested in the 'Why?'. Today, with the exception of Creationists, many Christians are happy to listen to cosmological theories and explore the dialogue between religion and science. Equally, there are many Christians who do not need to have Creation explained by science. This is not because they agree or disagree with cosmological theories, but because they accept with faith that God is the creator of the universe, as detailed in Genesis 1–2, and do not require proof of this.

Christianity teaches that the universe is important and has value because it has been created and proclaimed 'good' by God. It also teaches that God is omniscient and omnibenevolent and therefore knows and cares about everything that happens in the universe and intervenes in it.

Sources of authority

The heavens declare the glory of God;

the skies proclaim the work of his hands.

Day after day they pour forth speech;

night after night they reveal knowledge.

They have no speech, they use no words;

no sound is heard from them.

Yet their voice goes out into all the earth,

their words to the ends of the world…

(Psalms 19:1–4)

Sources of authority

Are not two sparrows sold for a penny? Yet not one of them will fall to the ground outside your Father's care. (Matthew 10:29)

The Incarnation of Jesus is believed to be God's intervention in the universe, as are miracles. Some Christians believe that the Incarnation and miracles are examples of **special revelations**. Special revelations are events and happenings, which made God's will and knowledge available to human beings as well as through **general revelation**.

Christians believe that the universe is a source of general revelation. General revelation is something that is believed to show the existence of God in an indirect way, through God's ongoing care of creation. For example, some Christians would argue that the existence of rain and the seasons are evidence of this as it provides all created beings with the water and food they need to survive. Another popular example is the Carbon Cycle, which is essential for life. Christianity teaches that humans can find evidence of God in the laws and nature of the physical universe. This is also sometimes referred to as **natural theology**, or knowledge about God from nature. One of the arguments for the existence of God is the 'Argument from Design' put forward by William Payley. Payley uses the example of the intricate mechanisms of a watch to argue that the universe is so complex there must have been someone like a 'watchmaker', namely God, who designed the universe and brought it into being.

Sources of authority

For since the creation of the world God's invisible qualities – his eternal power and divine nature have been clearly seen, being understood from what has been made… (Romans 1:20)

To Christians, this is saying that Creation is proof of God and you only have to look at what has been made (by God) to see/know God.

Responses to the view of the universe as a commodity

Christians have been criticised in the past for their attitude towards the universe. It has been argued that a literal interpretation of the Creation story, for example, Genesis 1:28 has led to the domination of the universe, specifically the Earth, by human beings who have seen it as a **commodity**, a resource to be used in any way that people want.

Sources of authority

God blessed them and said to them, 'Be fruitful and increase in number; fill the earth and subdue it. Rule over the fish in the sea and the birds in the sky and over every living creature that moves on the ground.' (Genesis 1:28)

In 1966 Lynn Townsend White, Jr, (1907–1987) a professor of medieval history wrote an important article called 'The Historical Roots of Our Ecological Crisis'. White argued that before the Industrial Revolution began in the 18th century people had a much more positive and interactive relationship with nature. The Industrial Revolution brought advances in science and technology that increased people's ability to destroy and exploit the environment. White believed that the attitude that the Earth was no more than a commodity for people to use could be found within the Christian religion. He thought that the Creation story had given rise to a human-centred, approach to the natural world. White also thought that Christian teaching had made an unhelpful distinction between human beings and the rest of creation, which was seen as having no 'soul' or the ability to reason and was therefore viewed as inferior. White felt that these beliefs had led to a lack of care for the environment, which still exists today. He suggested that the world should look to the life and teachings of St Francis of Assisi as a model for a more sustainable way of living.

One of the ways in which the Christian Church has responded to White's criticisms has been through the development of the idea of stewardship. The modern understanding of stewardship accepts that the resources of the Earth are there for humans to use but it emphasises that people have a moral and spiritual obligation to use these resources sustainably. Eco-justice strategies have also been adopted by the Worldwide Council of Churches and Christian ecological charities such as Christian Ecology Link and Operation Noah. An eco-justice strategy is something that protects the environment and also has a fair and positive impact socially and economically.

Activities ?

1. Make a list of all the ultimate questions you can think of that could follow on from: 'How did the universe come into being?' and try to answer them with a partner.
2. Design, draw and explain your own 'Cosmic Egg', which describes the Big Bang theory and the Theory of the Expanding Universe.
3. In groups, discuss whether you think it is fair to blame Christians for the ecological problems that exist today.

Can you remember?

- What does the Bible teach about the creation of the universe?
- What is Creationism?
- Why might Christians understand the Creation story differently?

Exam-style question

Outline three reasons why Lemaitre thought that there was no conflict between his cosmological theories as a scientist and his Christian faith. **(3 marks)**

Exam tip

Make sure that you understand and can explain Georges Lemaitre's contribution to cosmology and why he maintained that there was no conflict between scientific explanations for the beginning of the universe and Christian beliefs about Creation.

Summary

- Today, the idea now known as the Big Bang theory is the most accepted scientific explanation for how the universe came into being.
- Christianity teaches that the universe is important and is a reflection of God's great power and wisdom, known as general revelation.
- Many Christians believe that you can learn about God by studying the universe. This is known as natural theology.
- Christianity has been criticised in the past for encouraging a selfish and destructive attitude towards the environment. In response to this, the Christian Church has urged people to be better stewards of the Earth and the environment.

Checkpoint

Strengthen

S1 Who was Georges Lemaitre and why is his work considered important?

S2 Why do Christians believe that the universe is of value?

S3 Why have Christian attitudes towards the environment been criticised in the past?

Challenge

C1 Why might there be conflict between scientific and religious views about the origins of the universe and how could this be resolved?

C2 How could the 'Argument from Design' be used to prove the existence of God?

C3 How could better stewardship and eco-justice address the issue of the universe being seen as a commodity?

4.2 The sanctity of life

Learning objectives

- To understand Christian beliefs about the sanctity of life.
- To understand the importance of the sanctity of life for Christians today.

Sanctity of life

Christianity teaches that all life is special because it comes from God. Human life is believed to be particularly important to God and is regarded as holy or sacred because of this. Sanctity of life is a term used to describe the sacredness (or holiness) of human life. The Christian teaching that life is special and a belief in the sanctity of life is based on the teachings of the Bible.

Sources of authority

So God created mankind in his own image, in the image of God he created them;... (Genesis 1:27)

Then the Lord God formed a man from the dust of the ground and breathed into his nostrils the breath of life, and the man became a living being. (Genesis 2:7)

Christians believe that human life is different to all other forms of life because human beings are created in the image of God, as depicted in Genesis 1–3. Human beings also possess a soul given to them by God. This means that human life is precious, a gift from God that should not be violated. The value of human life is

Sources of authority

Before I formed you in the womb I knew you,

before you were born I set you apart;

I appointed you as a prophet to the nations. (Jeremiah 1:5)

For you created my inmost being;
*   you knit me together in my mother's womb.*

I praise you because I am fearfully and wonderfully made;
*   your works are wonderful,*
*   I know that full well.*

My frame was not hidden from you
*   when I was made in the secret place,*
*   when I was woven together in the depths of the earth.*

Your eyes saw my unformed body;
*   all the days ordained for me were written in your book*
*   before one of them came to be. (Psalms 139:13–16)*

reinforced by one of the Ten Commandments in the Bible that states 'Thou shalt not kill'. Christians also think that every human life is uniquely created and known by God, even before human beings are born. They also believe that God has a plan for everyone.

Bioethics

Christian beliefs about the sanctity of life are closely connected to an area of medical ethics known as

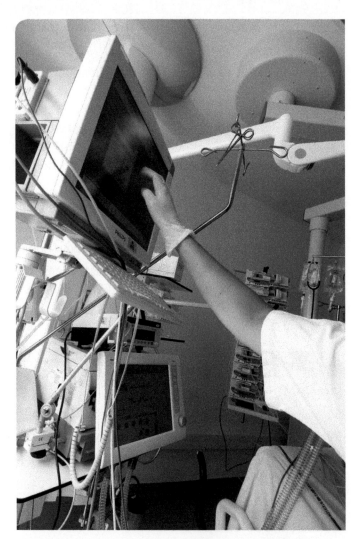

Figure 4.3 Advances in medicine and new technologies have brought a range of ethical issues, which need to be considered and managed by medical staff

bioethics. This is because bioethics is concerned with issues of right and wrong with regard to certain aspects of healthcare, particularly at the beginning and end of life. Abortion, embryo research, cloning, fertility treatments, genetic engineering and euthanasia are all examples of bioethical issues since they raise moral questions. For example, should people be kept alive by medical intervention no matter what the circumstances, even if they are permanently in great pain or are severely disabled? Does everyone have a right to have a child and access to fertility treatment if they need it? Is it right to have or carry out abortions? What are the implications of cloning and genetic engineering? Should human embryos be used in research? Who has the right to decide who lives and who dies? The sanctity of life can be an important consideration when discussing or debating bioethical issues.

Suicide and capital punishment are also matters of life and death associated with the sanctity of life.

Quality of life

The **quality of life** is sometimes discussed in relation to the sanctity of life, particularly with regard to bioethics. Quality of life means the overall well-being of someone; how comfortable are they, how good is their health, what is their life like in general in terms of the things human beings are believed to need in order to live a long and happy life? There are lots of different quality of life indicators that can be used to measure the general quality of a person's life. Health is an important indicator as living with pain or physical and mental problems can have a big impact on what a person's daily life is like. Poor health can also shorten people's lives. Some Christians believe that there are some circumstances in which an all-loving, omnibenevolent God would not want life to continue at all costs. For example, if someone was terminally ill, with no hope of a cure, and constantly in extreme pain, or so severely disabled that they had no quality of life whatsoever.

The importance of a belief in the sanctity of life for Christians today

A belief in the sanctity of life is an important Christian belief. This is significant for Christians today because it can have an impact on the way that a Christian might live their life, for example, Christians would try to live their life in a way that shows respect for all human life,

including their own. Some Christians do not overeat, drink alcohol, smoke or take drugs because they think that it is disrespecting God's gift of life. There are also Christians who become doctors and nurses or another kind of health professional because of their belief in the sanctity of life. They choose this as a career so they can help to preserve human life. It may also influence their attitude towards issues associated with the beginning and end of life, for example, abortion, embryo research, cloning, fertility treatments, genetic engineering, euthanasia, suicide and capital punishment. For some Christians decisions regarding these matters may be straightforward. For others, decisions may be more complex depending upon how they interpret and weigh up other Christian teachings, for example, the significance of agape and what the most loving thing to do is.

Christians believe that life is precious and a gift from God. While this might mean different things to individual Christians, all would agree this means they have a responsibility to make the most of their life and live it in the way that God wants. Many Christians would also try to find out what they believe is God's plan or purpose for them and try to follow that. Another impact of a belief in the sanctity of life is for Christians to try to live a life that shows respect for all things living, because God made them and gave them life. This may be difficult for some Christians to uphold in today's world and give rise to difficult questions that they would need to answer, for example, are abortion or euthanasia acceptable? It might also influence their views on suicide or capital punishment.

Activities	?

1 Write down the main things that you think people need in order to have a good quality of life, giving reasons for your responses.

2 In groups, discuss the following issues: abortion, embryo research, cloning, fertility treatments, genetic engineering and euthanasia. Identify why the sanctity of life might be a concern in each case.

3 'Sanctity of life is more important than quality of life'. Do you agree? Give reasons for your answer and consider how a Christian might respond to this statement.

Exam-style question

Explain two reasons why Christians believe in the sanctity of life. **(4 marks)**

Exam tip

Make sure you understand what the term sanctity of life means and why Christians believe in the sanctity of life.

Summary

- Christianity teaches that all life is special because it comes from God.
- Human life is believed to be particularly precious and is regarded as sacred.
- A belief in the sanctity of life can influence the way a Christian might try to live their life and their attitude towards bioethical issues associated with the beginning and end of life, such as abortion, embryo research, cloning, fertility treatments, genetic engineering and euthanasia.
- While all Christians may believe in the sanctity of life they can have different views about matters of life and death.

Checkpoint

Strengthen

S1 What does the term 'sanctity of life' mean?

S2 Why do Christians believe that human life is different to other forms of life?

S3 What is bioethics and how might it be connected with the sanctity of life?

Challenge

C1 How might a belief in the sanctity of life influence the life of a Christian?

C2 Why do you think some people might think that quality of life is more important than sanctity of life?

C3 How might a Christian try to find out what God's plan or purpose is for them?

4.3 The origins and value of human life

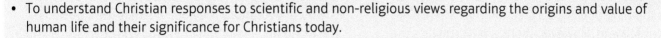

Learning objective

- To understand Christian responses to scientific and non-religious views regarding the origins and value of human life and their significance for Christians today.

The origins of human life

The study of human origins is called **anthropogeny**. The term comes from two ancient Greek words: *anthropos* meaning relating to humans and genesis, which means the process of creation or origin; *geny*, which stems from genesis, means the study of birth and gender of humans.

From a scientific perspective, it is difficult to establish exactly how life on Earth began, but it is thought to have developed or evolved very gradually over a long period of time. The Earth is believed to be approximately 4.5 billion years old, with life on Earth beginning about 3.8 billion years ago with single-celled micro-organisms like bacteria. Over the next billion years or so multi-cellular life evolved and diversified, but it is only in the last 570 million years that anything resembling the kind of life forms that we would recognise today came into being. Homo sapiens, the species to which human beings belong, have only been in existence for 200,000 years. This means that modern human beings have only been around for a very small part, 0.004%, of the Earth's history.

Evolution

The idea that life on Earth has evolved from common ancestors and diversified over a very long period of time is called evolution. Today, the theory of evolution is widely accepted by scientists as a way of explaining the wide range of life forms on Earth including how human beings came into existence.

Charles Darwin (1809–1882) was an English **naturalist**, someone who studies the natural world, who first put forward the theory of evolution. He explained his theory in a book called On the Origin of Species, which was published in 1859. Darwin's work was based on years of studying the natural world in lots of different environments across the world. He maintained that organisms gradually change and evolve into new species through 'natural selection'. **Natural selection** is the process where only those species that adapt the best to survive in their environment pass on their successful adaptations to following generations. This is sometimes referred to as 'the survival of the fittest'. Species that are poorly adapted to their environment do not survive and become extinct. For example, in the UK the peppered moth changed its colour from light to dark in London during the Industrial Revolution. It did this to survive as the soot from the factories made the trees darker, which meant that a lighter moth was more visible to predators. Darwin delayed publishing his work on evolution for 20 years because he knew it would be seen as scandalous in Victorian society, since the theory of evolution conflicted with Christian teaching and beliefs about Creation.

Darwin's book *On the Origin of Species* didn't deal with human evolution, but he did indicate that there was more to be said on the subject. In 1863 Thomas Huxley, an English biologist, published a book entitled *Evidence as to Man's Place in Nature*. Building on Darwin's earlier work, Huxley pointed out the similarities between humans and apes, arguing that humans had evolved from apes. People initially disagreed with his work as they thought that the human capacity to reason and make moral decisions couldn't be explained by natural selection. Darwin addressed these issues in *The Descent of Man*, and *Selection in Relation to Sex*, which was published in 1871.

Recent theories of human evolution argue that modern humans originated in Africa and migrated throughout the world, replaced older types of human species and continued to evolve into the modern type of human that exists today.

Christian responses to scientific theories about the origins of human life

In a special paper put forward by the Diocese of Manchester, the Church of England affirms that a belief in God and an understanding of science are compatible. This paper, entitled 'Special agenda IV

Diocesan Synod motions compatibility of science and Christian belief' points out that in modern times Christians have been at the forefront of scientific development, and many welcome the new understanding of all God's creation that Science has brought forward. However, there is nevertheless the potential for conflict.

Sources of authority

'Conflicts between science and religion arise on the one hand when religious views appear to reject or deny the findings of mainstream science. This is particularly acute when views, such as the claim that the earth is at most a few tens of thousand years old, are justified with scientific explanations which few support. They also arise when widespread scepticism and ignorance of scientific evidence in the population at large is blamed by scientists on religious belief.

On the other hand conflict also arises when scientists make claims which appear to be beyond what science can determine or claim that science is the only legitimate discipline that can resolve issues of existence, or that all will finally be revealed by the elusive 'Theory of everything'.

(Diocese of Manchester)

There is little doubt that modern scientific theories about the origins of human life and evolution do present a challenge to Christians today. When Darwin first published his work on evolution he said that it felt 'like confessing a murder' and there are people who have since argued that it was a murder – the murder of God! They say this because evolution seems to completely contradict the Christian Creation story in the Bible. For some Christians, as in Darwin's own experience, scientific views about the origins of humans may be a test of their faith that is either overcome or could lead to agnosticism, which means believing no one can ever know if God exists or not, or atheism instead. However, Christian attitudes towards the origins of human beings, Darwin and evolution can vary, depending upon the way that Christians interpret the Creation story in the Bible.

Christians understand the Creation story in different ways, according to whether or not they have a literal or non-literal approach to the Bible. Some Christians believe that the account of Creation as it appears in the Bible is an accurate account of what actually happened. This is known as creationism. Christians who believe in creationism, or creationists, do not believe in the theory of evolution. They believe that the creation of the world and everything in it took place in six calendar days, exactly as it says in the book of Genesis. This stems from the view that the Bible is the inspired word of God, which is never mistaken.

Many Christians do not believe in creationism and think that the Creation story is not meant to be taken literally. They believe that the six 'days' of creation are a metaphor for much longer periods of time and that the theory of evolution, like the Big Bang theory, is a description of the processes God used during Creation. Other Christians remain open-minded about scientific theories of the origins and evolution of human beings. They believe that God created the universe and everything in it, including people but accept that precise knowledge about the way in which this was done is above and beyond human understanding.

The significance of these responses for Christians today is that while Christians may have different views about scientific theories which seek to explain the origins and evolution of human beings, they share a common belief that ultimately God is responsible for the creation of the Earth and everything in it, including, and perhaps especially human beings. They further believe that human beings have a special place in God's creation and that every human being is known and loved by God. Christians believe that this means that every human life has value, meaning and purpose.

Christian responses to non-religious views on the value of human life

Scientific theories about the origins of human beings do not alter Christian views about the sanctity of human life. Christians share a respect for human life with people from other religions and agnostics and atheists alike. Most people, whether religious or not, would agree that human life is important and has value, although their reasons for thinking this might vary. The vast majority of people believe that human life has **intrinsic** value. This means that it is worth something in its own right just by existing. Christians would agree with this because they believe that human life is created in the image of God and that all human beings have a soul. Non-religious people might also agree that human life is intrinsically valuable but it would be for different reasons, such as human beings are capable of conscious thought and reason. Throughout the world human life is protected by international law and murder, the unlawful killing of someone, is wrong. This is testament to the fact that human life is believed to have intrinsic value and is important, regardless of whether or not it is believed to have been created by God.

Sources of authority

Everyone has the right to life, liberty and security of person. (Article 3 of the Universal Declaration of Human Rights).

There is an argument which says that all human rights are proof that human life is of intrinsic value. This is because human beings do not have to earn their basic human rights. They are the entitlement of every person regardless of their race, religion, gender, age, physical and mental abilities, etc. because they are of value in themselves. A belief in the intrinsic value of humanity whether based on religion or not is significant when considering beginning and end-of-life issues.

Human life is also regarded as having **extrinsic** value. This means that it has value in relation to other things such as its potential, for example, the things a person can do or achieve, or its connection to other things, for example, through relationships. Most Christians believe that fulfilling God's purpose for them gives their life greater meaning and value. They would also see it as important to let other humans know that their lives are of value to God, particularly people in difficult circumstances. The founding of Samaritans, which was originally a Christian charity, is an example of this. It would also be important for Christians to support the human rights of others, perhaps by campaigning against injustices or fundraising for charities like Christian Aid, which places the Universal Declaration of Human Rights at the core of its work.

Humanism, as the name suggests, affirms the worth of every human being. Humanists believe that the well-being and happiness of human beings is so important that they place it at the centre of their moral decision-making

process. They also accept that science can explain the origins of the universe and human life and reject the idea of the involvement of any supernatural being.

Figure 4.4 Charles Darwin's theory of the evolution of human beings

Activities ?

1. Explain whether you think evolution is proof of creation or proof that God does not exist, giving reasons for your answer.
2. Discuss with a partner how you think human beings came into existence, giving reasons for your answers.
3. Produce a piece of writing or a poem that explains what you think is the value of human life.

Can you remember?

- What do the terms sanctity of life and quality of life mean?
- What is bioethics?
- What is the significance of a belief in the sanctity of life for Christians today?

Exam-style question

Outline three reasons why a Christian might believe that human life is of intrinsic value. **(3 marks)**

Exam tip

Make sure you know the difference between intrinsic and extrinsic value and can express/say what Christians think about the value of human life.

Extend your knowledge

The Universal Declaration of Human Rights

The Universal Declaration of Human Rights is an internationally agreed document, which sets out the basic rights and freedoms that every human being is entitled to. The document consists of 30 articles or statements which cover a wide range of civil, cultural, economic, political and social rights. These rights are seen as universal to be enjoyed by people all over the world no matter who they are or where they live. The Universal Declaration of Human Rights was adopted by the United Nations in 1948 as a result of the concern of many countries about the experiences of the First and Second World Wars, and in particular how some people had been treated during the Second World War. It is not a treaty so it is not legally binding, but it has been very influential in developing international human rights law.

Summary

- Scientific theories argue that human beings were not created when the universe began billions of years ago but came into being much later through a process known as evolution.
- The theory of evolution was put forward by Charles Darwin in a book called *On the Origins of Species*.
- Scientific ideas about the origins of human beings do not affect the Christian belief in the sanctity of human life.
- Christians share a respect and regard for the value of human life with people from other religions and agnostics and atheists alike.
- The value of human beings is recognised in the Universal Declaration of Human Rights.

Checkpoint

Strengthen

S1 What is the theory of evolution?

S2 What challenges can scientific views about the origins of human life present to Christians today?

S3 Why do Christians believe that a human life has value?

Challenge

C1 Why might Christians find it difficult to reconcile an omnibenevolent and omniscient God with the theory of natural selection, i.e. only the fittest survive?

C2 What challenges could result from the Humanist idea of placing human well-being and happiness at the centre of moral decision-making?

C3 How does the existence of human rights support the idea that a human life is intrinsically valuable?

4.4 Abortion

4.4 Abortion

Learning objectives

- To understand the nature of abortion.
- To understand Christian teachings about abortion.
- To understand atheist and Humanist attitudes towards abortion and Christian responses to these views.

What is abortion?

Abortion is the medical process of terminating or ending a human pregnancy so that it does not result in the birth of a baby. An abortion is different to a miscarriage. A miscarriage is the spontaneous or natural ending of a pregnancy, which does not result in the birth of a live baby.

There are a number of reasons why a woman might want an abortion:
- very difficult personal circumstances
- health risk for the mother (mentally or physically)
- a high chance that the baby will be born with a serious abnormality.

Sources of authority

The law and abortion

Under UK law, an abortion can usually only be carried out during the first 24 weeks of pregnancy as long as certain criteria are met (see below).

The Abortion Act 1967 covers England, Scotland and Wales but not Northern Ireland, and states:

- *abortions must be carried out in a hospital or a specialist licensed clinic*
- *two doctors must agree that an abortion would cause less damage to a woman's physical or mental health than continuing with the pregnancy*

There are also a number of rarer situations when the law states an abortion may be carried out after 24 weeks. These include:

- *if it's necessary to save the woman's life*
- *to prevent grave permanent injury to the physical or mental health of the pregnant woman*
- *if there is substantial risk that the child would be born with serious physical or mental disabilities*

Generally, an abortion should be carried out as early in the pregnancy as possible, usually before 12 weeks and ideally before 9 weeks where possible.

(NHS Choices)

Pro-life and pro-choice

Generally, religious and non-religious attitudes fall into two categories: **pro-life** and **pro-choice**. Pro-life is against abortion: the foetus has a right to life. However, this does not mean pro-choice is pro-abortion. Pro-choice means that individuals have the right to decide whether or not abortion is the right choice for them. People who are pro-choice might be against abortion on a personal level but believe that women should have the right to choose whether abortion is the right choice for them.

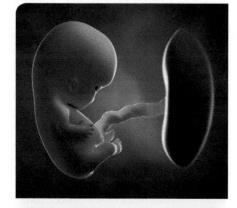
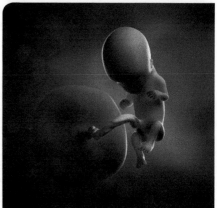

Figure 4.5 A foetus at 9, 12 and 24 weeks

Ensoulment

The issue of when human life is believed to begin is often closely connected to people's attitudes towards abortion. There has been a lot of debate among Christians about when human life begins, and as a consequence about whether the deliberate ending of a pregnancy could be considered 'taking a life', or even murder.

There has always been a variety of views within Christianity about when human life begins and whether there is a distinction between the start of biological life and the start of human life. This is because of **ensoulment**. The idea of ensoulment originally came from Aristotle, an ancient Greek philosopher. Aristotle (384–322 BCE) taught that a human embryo or foetus in the early stages of development initially had the soul of a vegetable, followed by the soul of an animal and only later through 'ensoulment' became 'animated' with a human soul.

Christianity teaches that ensoulment is when God introduces or places the soul into the embryo or foetus. The presence of the soul changes what was previously biological life (a collection of cells) and the foetus becomes a human life, which makes abortion unacceptable. Christians have different ideas about when ensoulment takes place. Some Christians believe that ensoulment happens at the moment of conception, whereas others believe it takes place later in the development of the embryo or foetus.

Different Christian attitudes towards abortion

The Bible does not specifically mention abortion but does form the basis of the Christian belief in the sanctity of life, which is relevant to this issue. Traditionally, a belief in the sanctity of life has meant that the Christian Church has been opposed to abortion and Christianity has taught that abortion is wrong. However, in the 1960s Christian attitudes towards abortion changed. This was in response to concerns about the impact of increasing numbers of illegal abortions on the health and well-being of women. Some Christians thought that the consequences of illegal abortion on society were a moral issue that could not be ignored. They believed that legalised abortion, under very strict circumstances, while still not believed to be a positive choice, would be more appropriate than seeking and undergoing an illegal abortion.

David Steele, the Member of Parliament who introduced the Abortion Bill to Parliament, was a Christian who maintained that he had no difficulty reconciling his Christianity with abortion law reform. His views were influenced by a document produced by the Church of England in 1965 entitled 'Abortion: An Ethical Discussion', within which the life of the mother as well as the unborn child is considered.

Sources of authority

To regard the life of the mother as less valuable than that of the unborn child does not consider her 'right to life' in terms of her wider roles of wife or mother (actual or potential) of other children, as well as in terms of her own person. (Abortion, an Ethical Discussion, Church information office, 1965)

Sources of authority

We affirm that every human life, created in the divine image, is unique… We therefore believe that abortion is an evil… and that abortion on demand would be a very great evil. But we also believe that to withdraw compassion is evil, and in circumstances of extreme distress or need, a very great evil… In an imperfect world the 'right' choice is sometimes the lesser of two evils. (The Church of England, 1988)

Today, the Church of England's view on abortion remains very much the same. It encourages its followers to think through the issue of abortion for themselves within the context of the Christian faith and in discussion with other Christians. The Church of England accepts that there will be differences of opinion between Christians on the issue of abortion but sets out its position with regard to abortion as follows:

The 'strictly limited' conditions under which abortion 'may be morally preferable' to any other alternative are if:

- there is a risk to the mother's life or her mental and physical health
- the baby is likely to have a serious disability and the mother feels she cannot cope
- the pregnancy arose as a result of rape.

The Church of England encourages a compassionate but serious and responsible approach towards abortion. Anglicans are urged to have 'compassion for the mother and a proper responsibility for the life of the unborn child'. The Church of England would also like to see abortion law

Sources of authority

The Church of England combines strong opposition to abortion with a recognition that there can be – strictly limited – conditions under which it may be morally preferable to any available alternative. (The Church of England)

applied more strictly and the number of abortions reduced. It believes that Christians can help towards this by providing every possible support for people who are pregnant in difficult circumstances, particularly through local church communities. This might include putting forward adoption as an alternative to abortion.

In contrast, the Catholic Church teaches that human life begins at the point of conception and abortion is murder. Abortion is always wrong no matter what the circumstances. The Catholic Church's traditional teaching on abortion was set out by Pope Paul VI in 1968 when he wrote an **encyclical**, a letter to all of the Catholic Bishops. The encyclical named *Humanae Vitae* is regarded as one of the Catholic Church's most important documents of modern times. It tells Catholics what the Church through **natural moral law** permits and forbids with regard to the regulation of procreation (the control of having children). Natural moral law is a set of principles established in nature by God, which can be used to decide whether human actions are right or wrong. Abortion goes against natural law. It disregards the fifth commandment 'Thou shalt not kill' and is considered a very grave sin against God.

Pope John Paul II, also took a very firm stance against abortion in 1995.

Many Catholic religious leaders recognise that the Church's teaching on abortion (and birth control) has political and social implications for society. It also emphasises another moral responsibility of the Catholic Church to ensure that every human being that is born has the best quality of life possible.

Not all Catholics agree with the Catholic Church's teaching on abortion. Abortion statistics show a contradiction in Catholic views about abortion. For while some Catholics believe that morally abortion is not a good choice they also accept that in some circumstances it may be the best or least bad moral choice. As a consequence of this some Catholics do have abortions.

Situation ethics
Christian attitudes towards abortion (and other issues where difficult moral decisions need to be made) can be influenced by a philosophical idea known as

---

Sources of authority

I declare that direct abortion, that is, abortion willed as an end or as a means, always constitutes a grave moral disorder, since it is the deliberate killing of an innocent human being.
(Pope John Paul II, Evangelium Vitae, 62, 1995)

---

situation ethics. This is where the circumstances of each individual situation are considered very carefully and Christians make a decision about whether something is morally right or wrong based on the principle of agape and what the most loving thing to do is for everyone involved.

Humanist and atheist views towards abortion
Humanists believe that abortion can be a morally acceptable choice. The Humanist movement campaigned for legalised abortion in the 1960s. Humanists do not believe that all life is sacred but they do respect and value life. They also think that quality of life is just as, if not more, important than a right to life. Most Humanists think that a foetus does not become a person at conception and that this happens later in the foetus' development. Humanists would probably tend to put the interests of the woman ahead of the foetus but think that all possible options, including adoption, should be explored before deciding on abortion. Most Humanists believe that abortion should be a last resort. They recognise that the decision to have an abortion is likely to be a very difficult one and that in an ideal world every child would be a wanted child. Humanists believe that the best way to avoid unwanted children and reduce the need for abortion is through improving sex education, providing more easily available contraception and better education and enhanced opportunities for women.

There is no single or definitive atheist view on abortion. Atheists may agree or disagree with abortion depending upon their personal beliefs. The Society for the Protection of Unborn Children notes that atheists can have very strong pro-life views.

In addition to being pro-life anti-choice, atheists can also be pro-choice but anti-abortion or pro-choice and pro-abortion.

Christian responses to Humanist and atheist views
Christians believe approach abortion from a religious perspective with a belief in the sanctity of human life. Although many atheists and Humanists approach abortion from a non-religious viewpoint, they also affirm the value of human life. As a consequence, there may be some agreement between certain Christian, atheist and Humanist views on abortion within the context of 'pro-life and anti-abortion' or 'pro-choice and anti-abortion' stances. All Christians, however, would disagree strongly with the views of those who are both pro-choice and pro-abortion.

Activities

1   In pairs, discuss and list the possible reasons a woman might have for wanting an abortion, whether you think they are valid or not. What alternatives might there be for each situation?

2   Think about what you have learned in this topic. Look again at the foetal development timeline and explain when you think life begins and why you think this.

3   In groups, role-play the following people having a discussion about abortion:
    - a pro-life Catholic
    - a pro-choice/anti -abortion Anglican
    - a pro-choice Humanist
    - a pro-choice/pro-abortion atheist.

Set aside a few minutes to prepare your arguments in relation to your role before you begin the discussion.

Exam-style question

Explain two different Christian teachings about abortion. **(4 marks)**

Exam tip

Make sure you know and can describe the Church of England's and the Catholic Church's teaching on abortion.

Summary

- Abortion is the medical process that terminates or ends a human pregnancy so that it does not result in the birth of a baby.
- Traditionally, the Christian Church has taught that abortion is wrong in all circumstances.
- Today, denominations have different views and for many Christians it is a very complex issue.
- Humanists believe that abortion is a serious moral issue. They support a woman's right to have an abortion, if that is the right choice for them, but believe that abortion should be a last resort.
- Atheists have differing views about abortion. Some atheists are very pro-life and totally against abortion, whereas others believe that it can be a positive moral choice.
- A Christian may or may not share the views of an atheist or Humanist about abortion, depending upon each of their personal beliefs. Most Christians would disagree with the idea that abortion can be a positive moral choice.

Checkpoint

Strengthen

S1   What is abortion and how is it different to a miscarriage?

S2   What does the law say about abortion?

S3   What does Christianity teach about abortion?

Challenge

C1   Why might Christians have different views about abortion?

C2   What is the difference between a pro-life and pro-choice attitude towards abortion?

C3   How might Christians respond to atheist and Humanist views about abortion?

4.5 Death and the afterlife

Life after death

What happens when we die? Is there life after death? These are two important questions that many people would like to know the answer to. They are very difficult questions to answer: human beings might know what happens biologically when people die; but no one knows for certain what, if anything, happens beyond that. Many people believe that 'life' does continue in some form after death. Equally there are people who believe that there is nothing beyond death; it is the end of human or any other kind of existence.

People who do believe in life after death can have very different ideas about what the afterlife is like. Some think that life after death continues in a spiritual type realm, such as heaven and hell, whereas others believe that individuals are reborn into this world and experience successive cycles of birth, death and rebirth, known as **reincarnation**. There are also people who believe in the idea of an afterlife but don't really have a clear idea or vision of what it might be.

People might believe in life after death for a variety of reasons. They may hold this belief for religious reasons. Alternatively, it may be because they, or someone they know, has experienced something extraordinary, like a near-death experience; or they think they can remember a previous existence, as in the case of 'remembered lives', which they believe proves there is something beyond death. Another reason why someone might have a belief in life after death is because they cannot accept that a single lifetime on Earth is all that there is. Some people argue that there is energy associated with a human life, perhaps in the form of the soul, which cannot be destroyed on death. It could also be that people find it emotionally comforting to think that there is a possibility of being reunited in an afterlife with loved ones who have died. The idea of an afterlife might also seem appealing because it is where the consequences of good and bad behaviour or the unfairness of human life are ultimately addressed.

Christian teachings and beliefs about life after death

Christianity teaches that life has a purpose and that death isn't the end of our existence. Christians believe that the resurrection of Jesus and his later ascension into heaven proved that there is life after death. They also believe it means that Christians have the opportunity to be with God in heaven after death (see also salvation and Atonement Chapter 1, p 21 (Topic 1.5)).

Sources of authority

As for you, you were dead in your transgressions and sins, in which you used to live when you followed the ways of this world and of the ruler of the kingdom of the air, the spirit who is now at work in those who are disobedient. All of us also lived among them at one time, gratifying the cravings of our flesh and following its desires and thoughts. Like the rest, we were by nature deserving of wrath. But because of his great love for us, God, who is rich in mercy, made us alive with Christ even when we were dead in transgressions – it is by grace you have been saved. And God raised us up with Christ and seated us with him in the heavenly realms in Christ Jesus, in order that in the coming ages he might show the incomparable riches of his grace, expressed in his kindness to us in Christ Jesus. For it is by grace you have been saved, through faith—and this is not from yourselves, it is the gift of God— not by works, so that no one can boast. For we are God's handiwork, created in Christ Jesus to do good works, which God prepared in advance for us to do. (Ephesians 2:1–10)

Many Christians refer to death as a physical death. This is because they believe that the soul of a human being is immortal, which means the soul cannot die or be destroyed. Christians believe that the soul has a consciousness. It leaves the body at death and continues to exist in the afterlife: either in heaven or hell. Christians believe that the destination of the soul is dependent upon whether or not it has attained salvation. Souls that have been saved from the consequences of their sins will go to heaven, whereas, the souls that have not achieved salvation will need to accept the consequences of their sins. They will be judged by God and sentenced to spend eternity in hell. Christians believe that the judgement of God will decide the destination of the soul after death and at the end of the world or 'end times'.

Figure 4.6 Easter Morning, He Qi, a Chinese artist living in the USA, is a popular artist who specialises in religious themes. In this image of the Resurrection an angel announces that Christ has risen, and the demons of darkness are fleeing from him. The women have not yet woken properly, and seem unaware of what has happened. He Qi's angel carries a simple white lily, a sign of purity and peace

Heaven

Traditionally, Christians have understood heaven to be a transcendent, spiritual realm rather than a physical place in the universe. The Bible teaches that there is no sin, sadness, pain or suffering in heaven. Christians understand this to mean that heaven is a holy, happy and peaceful state of being with God and Jesus after death. In Christian art, there have been lots of paintings depicting heaven, but Christians agree that it is very difficult to accurately describe heaven. This is because no one knows what heaven is like, since it is beyond all human experience. Even people who are believed to have undergone near-death experiences have been unable to provide accurate accounts of what they believe heaven is like.

Sources of authority

'He will wipe every tear from their eyes. There will be no more death' or mourning or crying or pain, for the old order of things has passed away.' (Revelation, 21:4)

Hell

Christianity teaches that hell is a place or state of being where unrepentant sinners go after death. An unrepentant sinner is someone who does not regret the things they have done wrong and refuses God's offer of forgiveness and salvation through Jesus. A well-known image of hell, as an underground, subterranean place of eternal fire and suffering where body and soul could be destroyed, is based on the literal interpretation of biblical ideas. However, many Christians today believe that hell is not being in the presence of God after death. They think that the soul after death will long to be reunited with God, who created it and in whose image it was made. Therefore, the punishment and misery of hell is being apart from God. Hell is seen to be spiritual desolation or isolation of the soul.

Sources of authority

Do not be afraid of those who kill the body but cannot kill the soul. Rather, be afraid of the One who can destroy both soul and body in hell. (Matthew, 10:28)

Purgatory

The Orthodox and Roman Catholic Churches teach that there is also an intermediate state after physical death known as Purgatory. This is a place where souls are purified in order to be holy enough to enter heaven. Christians who believe in this idea think that that the time a soul spends in Purgatory can be shortened by the prayers of those still alive. While other denominations, like Anglicans, may not refer to it as Purgatory they also believe that the soul continues to develop and grow in holiness after death.

Atheist and Humanist beliefs about life after death

Atheists do not believe in life after death or the idea of an afterlife. They think that we only live once and reject the idea of an immortal soul. Richard Dawkins, a very prominent atheist, maintains that humans are a product of evolution and not a unique creation of God; human beings are just composed of chemicals and that individuality is a result of genetics. Dawkins argues that evolution has enabled human beings to develop a consciousness so they can choose behaviour most likely to help their survival. He says that this consciousness resides inside the brain of a human being, which ceases to exist after death. Dawkins believes that while the idea of an afterlife may bring comfort to a huge number of people, there is no reason other than 'wishful thinking' or something akin to 'magical thinking' to suggest that consciousness can survive physical death. Dawkins accepts that there are many things that we, as human beings, do not yet really know '… how the universe works… there are many things we don't understand, but the particular thing of surviving our own death [is] palpable wishful thinking that goes against everything we understand about how the nervous system works…we are apes, we are African apes.'

Humanists also believe that we only live once and reject the idea of a life after death. They believe that the only way we live on is through what we have achieved while we are alive; the memories people have of us and through our children, if we have them. Humanists say that the fact that there is no afterlife makes our lives on Earth even more precious.

Reincarnation and remembered lives

Eastern religions like Hinduism believe in the **transmigration** of the soul after death. Transmigration means that the soul passes from one body to another after death. It is also known as reincarnation. There are people who claim to remember very precise details of the life or lives they have led previously, which they then claim can be verified independently. In some cases, it is claimed that children have birth marks or physical defects that correspond with what they believe to be their often abrupt and violent death in a previous life. Many people take these accounts of remembered lives seriously. They believe that they are evidence of reincarnation and the existence

Figure 4.7 A Hindu reincarnation ceremony

Sources of authority

We can seem very small and insignificant when we think about the vast size and age of the universe. Some people think that if there is no life after death life is somehow meaningless and pointless. But our individual lives and feelings are still important to us, and something that comes to an end is not necessarily meaningless – it can be all the more precious. Humanists have to create their own meanings for their lives, without any illusions about their own importance in the grand scheme of things or any concern for reward or punishment after death. The main thing is to try to be happy now, while we are alive, and to make other people happy. We don't get another chance…

The stark truth is that life isn't 'for' anything, it just is; there is no underlying purpose to it all. But human beings have the great privilege of intelligence, imagination, creativity – we can give our own lives a sense of direction and purpose. We may have many worthwhile purposes and projects that make us feel that life is worth living; there doesn't have to be just one purpose (for example, to do God's will). (humanismforschools.org.uk)

of life after death in the form of the transmigration of the soul. Not everyone believes that accounts of remembered lives are true. People who don't believe in reincarnation might argue that stories of remembered lives are fraudulent accounts put together by people to attract attention or make money.

Near-death experiences

A near-death experience (NDE) is a personal and paranormal experience in which someone very close to death is apparently outside of their body and is aware of what is happening. NDEs have been the subject of lots of research and some common features have been identified. Many people who claim to have had a NDE report experiencing an extreme sense of peace and well-being. They often say that they are drawn towards or enveloped in a powerful white light and/or 'see' loved ones who are deceased, or caring beings dressed in white. Others state that they have seen their own body and doctors and nurses trying to resuscitate them, or they sense that they are moving upwards, going through a tunnel, entering a darkness or travelling through a passageway. Another common feature is that people undergoing NDEs believe that they have a choice to make about returning to their body; not dying and carrying on with their human life. Many people take NDE accounts seriously and researchers have found that the things experienced are connected with an individual's cultural beliefs, including their religion. Some people argue that there is a scientific or logical explanation for NDEs, whereas others believe that they are proof that there is life after death. There is little doubt that for people who believe that they have undergone a NDE it is a life-changing experience.

Christian responses to non-religious arguments against an afterlife

People who follow other religions and people who are not religious would disagree with Christian beliefs about life after death. They would disagree because they hold different beliefs about what happens after death, including the belief that there is no kind of afterlife whatsoever. Christians reject all arguments that say that there is no life after death. This is because they have faith in the resurrection of Jesus, which they believe proves that there is life after death. They also believe in the teachings of Jesus, recorded in the Bible, which say that he is the key to eternal life and that through a belief in Jesus they too will have eternal life.

The basis for Christian beliefs about life after death have been criticised by the non-religious. Some of the arguments put forward are that there is a lack of evidence to prove the resurrection of Jesus actually took place and the accounts of the resurrection are at worst fraudulent and at best a comforting idea that has no real merit. Another argument is that the idea of going to heaven and hell, after death acts as a form of social control by the Church, as it influences the way that Christians behave.

In 1 Peter 3:15–22 Christians are taught that they must be prepared to explain what they believe about the afterlife to the non-religious and why they believe it. They should do this in a gentle and reasoned way, using the way they live their life (through faith in Jesus) and the Bible as examples to support their beliefs about life after death. Hell, after death acts as a form of social control by the Church, as it influences the way that Christians behave.

Sources of authority

But in your hearts revere Christ as Lord. Always be prepared to give an answer to everyone who asks you to give reason for the hope that you have. But do this with gentleness and respect, keeping a clear conscience, so that those who speak maliciously against your good behaviour in Christ may be ashamed of their slander. For it is better, if it is God's will, to suffer for doing good than for doing evil. For Christ also suffered once for sins, the righteous for the unrighteous, to bring you to God. He was put to death in the body but made alive in the Spirit. After being made alive, he went and made proclamation to the imprisoned spirits— to those who were disobedient long ago when God waited patiently in the days of Noah while the ark was being built. In it only a few people, eight in all, were saved through water, and this water symbolizes baptism that now saves you also—not the removal of dirt from the body but the pledge of a clear conscience toward God. It saves you by the resurrection of Jesus Christ, who has gone into heaven and is at God's right hand—with angels, authorities and powers in submission to him. (1 Peter 3:15–22)

Can you remember?

- Why might abortion be regarded as a bioethical issue?
- What does the law say about abortion?
- What does Christianity teach about abortion?

Activities   ?

1 Summarise why Christians believe that there is life after death.
2 Based on the information in this topic, your wider general knowledge and personal opinions, create a table containing arguments for and against life after death.
3 Write a poem or a piece of writing entitled either 'Death is not the end' or 'Death is the end.'

Exam tip

Ensure that you know and are able to explain Christian beliefs about the afterlife. Make sure that you can support your statements with at least one source of wisdom and authority.

Extend your knowledge

In the Bible, in 1 Corinthians, St Paul teaches that after death Christians will be resurrected, like Jesus. Their human body will also be transformed from a physical body to a spiritual body.

So will it be with the resurrection of the dead. The body that is sown is perishable, it is raised imperishable; it is sown in dishonour, it is raised in glory; it is sown in weakness, it is raised in power; it is sown a natural body, it is raised a spiritual body.

If there is a natural body, there is also a spiritual body. (1 Corinthians, 15:42–44)

Exam-style question

Explain two Christian beliefs about the afterlife.
You must refer to a source of wisdom and authority in your answer. **(5 marks)**

Summary

- People have different ideas about what happens after death.
- Christians believe that the resurrection of Jesus proves that life continues after death.
- Atheists and Humanists do not believe in life after death. They argue that death is the end of human existence and to think anything else is just 'wishful thinking'.
- Christians reject all arguments that say there is no such thing as an afterlife. They are also taught to answer questions and explain their beliefs to the non-religious.
- Some people claim to have had near death experiences, which they think supports the idea of an afterlife, although others disagree and say that this can be explained in other ways.

Checkpoint

Strengthen

S1 What does Christianity teach about death?
S2 How do Christians understand the concept of the afterlife?
S3 Why is Jesus important to a Christian belief in life after death?

Challenge

C1 Why might people argue that there is no such thing as life after death?
C2 How have Christian beliefs about life after death been criticised and how are Christians taught to respond to this? Or what arguments have people put forward against Christian beliefs about life after death and how are Christians taught to respond to criticism of their beliefs?
C3 In what ways could a paranormal experience like an NDE be a life changing experience?

4.6 Euthanasia

Learning objectives

- To understand Christian teachings and beliefs about euthanasia.
- To understand atheist and Humanist attitudes towards euthanasia and Christian responses to these views.
- To understand Christian support for hospice care as an alternative to euthanasia.

What is euthanasia?

Euthanasia is a term used to describe the act of ending a person's life, or allowing them to die, in order to relieve pain and suffering. It can also be referred to as **assisted dying**. The word euthanasia comes from the Greek word *euthanatos* and means 'good' or 'easy' death. A person who undergoes euthanasia is usually extremely ill with an incurable condition. There are also other situations where someone might want their life to be ended. In many cases, euthanasia is carried out at the person's request. This is called **voluntary euthanasia**. There are several circumstances that could be classed as voluntary euthanasia, such as:

- someone asking for help to end their life
- declining potentially life-saving treatment, including resuscitation
- refusing to eat or drink
- requesting medical treatment is stopped, or life support machines are switched off.

At other times, a person may be too ill to communicate their wishes and the decision is made by their next of kin and/or other relatives, health professionals or the courts. This is called **non-voluntary euthanasia**. For example, the decision by relatives to switch off a life-support machine of someone who is in a coma could result in non-voluntary euthanasia.

Some people prepare a **living will** in case they become ill and cannot communicate their wishes. A living will is a document that sets out how you want to be treated and cared for in the event of particular circumstances, but are unable to let people know this at the time. A living will is not legally binding, but it could be taken into consideration when determining treatment and care for someone who is unable to say what they want to happen.

The way that euthanasia is carried out can either be actively or passively. **Active euthanasia** is when someone such as a medical professional deliberately does something to make the patient die, such as giving them a lethal dose of drugs. **Passive euthanasia** happens when death of the patient occurs because someone such as a doctor does not do something that is necessary to keep them alive or when they stop doing something that is keeping the patient alive, such as not carrying out artificial respiration on a terminally ill patient or switching off a life-support machine.

Euthanasia is a complex moral issue and people can have very different views on the issue regardless of whether they are religious or not. Many people make a moral distinction between active and passive euthanasia. They say that there is a massive difference between deliberately killing a patient and withholding treatment to let them die. Some people, like doctors, nurses and close relatives, may prefer the idea of passive euthanasia to active euthanasia. This is because they could fulfil the wishes of a very ill patient who does not want to prolong their life and wishes to die without deliberately killing them. 'Do not resuscitate' requests are an example of passive euthanasia.

Others might argue that letting someone die as opposed to deliberately killing them might make people feel better but it is still wrong. This is because they believe that human beings, particularly medical professionals, have a responsibility to preserve and save lives whenever they can. They may also say that morally the distinction between active and passive euthanasia is meaningless because they both still involve a deliberate decision either to do or not to do something, which results in the death of another person, albeit for compassionate reasons. There are also people who say that active euthanasia is more humane than passive euthanasia, as passive euthanasia can result in a much slower and more painful death for people.

The law and euthanasia

Euthanasia can be considered as manslaughter or murder, depending upon the circumstances. It is illegal in the UK and in most other countries in the world. Albania, Belgium, the Netherlands and Switzerland are among the very few countries that have laws allowing euthanasia.

In September 2015 there was an attempt to change the law on euthanasia in the UK through the presentation of the Assisted Dying Bill. This was rejected by Parliament.

Dignity in Dying

Dignity in Dying is a national membership organisation that campaigns to make assisted dying, euthanasia, a legal option for 'terminally ill, mentally competent adults' in the UK. They believe that subject to certain safeguards, 'everyone has the right to a dignified death', which means that each individual should have:

- Choice over where we die, who is present and our treatment options.
- Access to expert information on our options, good quality end-of-life care, and support for loved ones and carers.
- Control over how we die, our symptoms and pain relief, and planning our own death.
  (Source: http://www.DignityinDying.org.uk/)

Dignity in Dying maintains that there needs to be a change in the law to prevent dying people suffering against their wishes at the end of their life; and making decisions without having proper advice from healthcare professionals. It would also prevent dying people trying to take matters into their own hands, perhaps trying to persuade their families to help them. They say that people who can afford to currently travel abroad to countries where euthanasia is legal to end their lives. Approximately one person a fortnight is thought to go to Switzerland to do this.

Different Christian teachings about euthanasia

The Bible does not specifically mention euthanasia. However, it does underpin the Christian belief in the sanctity of life, which is relevant to this issue. Most Christians are opposed to euthanasia or assisted dying.

Christianity teaches that human life is precious, a gift from God which should not be violated. The value of human life is reinforced by one of the Ten Commandments, in the Bible, which states 'Thou shalt not kill'. They also believe

that God has a plan for everyone and that good and bad (trouble) and birth and death are part of that plan. Only God who created life has the authority to end life no matter how bad the circumstances might be.

Some Christians believe this idea is illustrated in the book of Job in the Bible, which describes a time of extreme pain and suffering experienced by Job and his wife. In Job 2:1-8, Satan challenges God by claiming that a man will give up eventually if he suffers enough pain. God gives Satan permission to test this theory on Job. After Job is burdened with pain all over his body, Job's wife suggests he give up and curse God for their suffering. However, Job argues that his life has always been in God's hands and, because they have received both good and bad from God in the past, he trusts in God's will. As a result, Job maintains his integrity as a servant of God and does not fall into the trap set by Satan by giving up or taking his own life.

Sources of authority

His wife said to him, 'Are you still maintaining your integrity? Curse God and die!'
He replied, 'you are talking like a foolish woman. Shall we accept good from God, and not trouble?' In all this Job did not sin in what he said. (Job 2:9–10)

The Church of England is strongly opposed to euthanasia. The Church's most recent position on this issue is set out in its opposition to the Assisted Dying Bill in 2015.

Sources of authority

Vulnerable individuals must be cared for and protected even if, at times, this calls for sacrifice on the part of others… We must choose what sort of society we wish to become: one in which people are valued primarily for their utility or one in which every person is supported, protected and cherished even if, at times, they fail to cherish themselves… Better access to high-quality, holistic palliative care, greater support for carers and enhanced end of life services are the hallmarks of a truly compassionate society and it is to those ends that our energies must be directed.

(Rev Dr Brendan McCarthy, The Church of England national adviser on medical ethics)

Similarly, the Roman Catholic Church teaches that euthanasia is morally wrong. Pope John Paul II referred

Figure 4.8 Whose life is it anyway? Is voluntary euthanasia a morally correct choice?

Sources of authority

…Humanist concern for quality of life and respect for personal autonomy lead to the view that in many circumstances voluntary euthanasia is the morally right course. People should have the right to choose a painless and dignified end, either at the time or beforehand, perhaps in a 'living will'. The right circumstances might include: extreme pain and suffering; helplessness and loss of personal dignity; permanent loss of those things which have made life worth living for this individual… Individuals should be allowed to decide on such personal matters for themselves. While humanists generally support voluntary euthanasia, they also uphold the need for certain safeguards. These may include counselling, the prevention of pressure on patients, clear witnessed instructions from the patient, the involvement of several doctors, no reasonable hope of recovery. (British Humanist Association)

to it as 'a grave violation of the law of God'. However, people have a right to refuse aggressive and extraordinary medical treatments if they wish to. They may also take medicines such as painkillers that could shorten their life providing the aim is to relieve pain and not to hasten death. This is known as the **Doctrine of Double Effect**. The Doctrine of Double Effect is when something morally good, such as giving pain relief, has an unwanted side effect which is morally bad: the death of the patient.

The Roman Catholic Church sets out the Churches formal teaching on euthanasia in the Catechism of the Roman Catholic Church. The **Catechism** is an explanation of Catholic beliefs based on the Bible and the traditions of the Roman Catholic Church.

Humanist and atheist attitudes towards euthanasia

Generally, Humanists support voluntary euthanasia. They believe that under some circumstances, subject to certain safeguards, it may be morally the right thing to do. Humanists do not believe in God so they do not believe that only God can decide when and how people die. Many atheists would also agree with this view. Humanists and atheists believe human beings have a fundamental right to die with dignity in a way that they have chosen.

Christian responses to these views

Most Christians would disagree with Humanist and atheist views about euthanasia. This is because they believe in the sanctity of life. Life is a gift from God. Only God who created life can take life away. Free will does not give human beings the right to take away life, not even their own. Christians argue that everyone's life is of value to God even in the midst of pain and suffering. They also believe that stewardship means that they have a responsibility to protect the weak and vulnerable in society. Many Christians think that legalising voluntary euthanasia could mean that people feel pressured to end their lives so they are not a burden to their family; a 'right to die becomes a duty to die!'. It could also eventually lead to involuntary euthanasia being seen as acceptable.

Hospice care

Most Christians and non-Christians who disagree with euthanasia would support **hospice care** as an alternative to assisted dying. The purpose of hospice care is to improve the quality of life for people who have an incurable illness and it is often provided by charities. It is a particular style of care, which aims to meet all of the medical, emotional, social, practical, psychological and spiritual needs of the person who is ill, plus the needs of the person's family and carers. Hospice care can begin when a person is first diagnosed as being terminally ill and ends when they die. It can take place at home or in another setting such as a care home or a purpose-built hospice. You may have a hospice near your school or where you live. People who disagree with euthanasia argue that hospice care can provide a suitable alternative.

Hospice care does not have to be continuous. People may feel that they can take a break from hospice care if their condition is stable and they are feeling all right. Hospices can also provide what is known as respite care for a terminally ill person if their carers need a break or are unable to care for them for a short time. Hospice care also includes palliative care. Palliative care is medical care that provides people who are terminally ill with relief from their symptoms, pain and physical and mental stress.

The modern hospice care movement was founded by a Christian, Dame Cecily Saunders, who established St Christopher's Hospice in south west London. She also initiated the idea of palliative care.

Activities ?

1   Spend a few minutes making sure you can correctly spell and know the meaning of all the key terms in this topic. Ask a partner to test you on them. Learn any that you get wrong for homework!

2   In groups, design a hospice facility as an alternative to euthanasia, explaining the features you have chosen and why you have included them.

3   Write an article from a Christian perspective, explaining why you are pleased that the Assisted Dying Bill 2015 was rejected by Parliament.

Exam-style question

Explain two reasons why most Christians are opposed to euthanasia.

You must refer to a source of wisdom and authority in your answer. **(5 marks)**

Exam tip

Ensure that you understand and can explain the key Christian arguments against euthanasia and are able to support your statements with at least one source of wisdom and authority.

Can you remember?

- What is a remembered life?
- Why do some people regard near death experiences as proof that there is life after death?
- How might Christians respond to non-religious arguments against life after death?

Summary

- Euthanasia is a term used to describe the deliberate act of ending a person's life to relieve pain and suffering. It is a complex issue and can also be known as assisted dying.
- Hospices and palliative care are seen as alternatives to euthanasia.
- Most Christians disagree with euthanasia and think it is morally wrong. This is because of a belief in the sanctity of life.
- Humanists and many atheists would like to see voluntary euthanasia legalised, under strict conditions. They believe that it is everyone's basic human right to be able to choose how and when they die.
- Christians do not want euthanasia to be legalised.

Checkpoint

Strengthen

S1 What is euthanasia?

S2 Why are Christians opposed to euthanasia and what might they put forward as an alternative?

S3 What arguments do people put forward in favour of euthanasia?

Challenge

C1 What kind of safeguards do you think Dying with Dignity might want to see put in place if assisted dying was made legal?

C2 Why do you think some people say that making voluntary euthanasia legal in the UK would open the doors/pave the way for the legalisation or downgrading of the criminal act of involuntary euthanasia?

C3 How might the Doctrine of Double Effect be applied to abortion?

4.7 Christian responses to issues in the natural world

Learning objectives

- To understand Christian beliefs about stewardship.
- To understand Christian responses to environmental issues.
- To understand Christian responses to animal rights issues.

Sources of authority

The present challenges of environment and economy, of human development and global poverty, can only be faced with extraordinary Christ-liberated courage.

Actions have to change for words to have effect.

(The Archbishop of Canterbury, Justin Welby)

Figure 4.9 Churches and individual Christians are encouraged to reduce their carbon footprint in four main ways by:

- improving energy efficiency in church buildings and in their homes
- making sustainable choices with regard to food, travel and other purchases in churches and their homes
- making church buildings and their homes sustainable by using sources of renewable energy
- developing the biodiversity of churchyards and the gardens in their homes.

Stewardship

Christians believe that stewardship is a way of life. It means living in a way that recognises that everything belongs to God. This means committing their life to God's service and being prepared to be held accountable for how they have used the abilities, resources and opportunities that God has given them. Christians believe that if they are good stewards God will reward them.

In the past, Christianity has been criticised for its attitude towards the Earth and the natural world. Today, many Christians believe that **environmentalism** is an appropriate response to the issue of stewardship. Environmentalism is concerned with the protection and improvement of the environment. This was echoed by the actions of HRH Prince Phillip and WWF International who, in 1986, called together leading members of five of the major world religions to discuss the importance of saving the natural world. Together they produced the Assisi Declarations of Nature, a set of key statements on each religion's beliefs about the Earth and commitment to environmental conservation.

Green Christianity is a term that is used to refer to Christians from all denominations who celebrate and protect the environment. Green Christians believe that it is important for humanity to recognise the difference between the stewardship and the ownership of the Earth. They oppose policies and practices that threaten the environment and the survival of the planet. Green Christian is also the name of a Christian environmental charity.

Shrinking the Footprint

Shrinking the Footprint is the Church of England's national environment campaign focusing on the issue of climate change. The Archbishop of Canterbury and leader of the Church of England, Justin Welby, believes that actions must change if environmental issues like climate change are to be addressed. He argues that Christians have an important role to play in decreasing the amount of pollution by reducing Carbon emissions (CO_2) into the atmosphere, which contributes to global warming.

Throughout the Church of England there are many examples of churches that are shrinking their footprint. For example, many churches have placed solar panels on their roofs and replaced old boilers with ground source heat pumps.

Operation Noah

Operation Noah is an ecumenical Christian charity, which means it represents many different churches. It is focused on addressing the growing threat of global warming and climate change. One of the ways it does this is by equipping churches with the resources to respond to these issues from providing materials that can be used during worship to giving talks on climate science.

A key initiative for Operation Noah, called 'Bright Now', is to try to help reduce the amounts of pollution in the atmosphere by getting churches not to use fossil fuels and invest in cleaner forms of energy instead.

Operation Noah also works with other environmental charities, such as Green Christian and People and Planet, which campaign to end world poverty, defend human rights and protect the environment.

While many Christians may be committed to protecting the environment, some Christians believe that the Church should get not involved in politics. Others think that getting involved in politics and getting governments to pass more environmentally friendly laws or impose penalties for environmental damage caused by big companies is the only way to secure positive and lasting environmental changes. An example of this is the change in English law in 2015 requiring all large shops in England to charge 5p for all single-use plastic carrier bags. The government did this to reduce the impact of carrier bag litter on the environment.

Figure 4.10 Operation Noah

Sources of authority

Christians who care about climate change can bear witness by ensuring they tread lightly on the earth through reducing their consumption and adopting a sustainable lifestyle. But acting on climate change goes beyond what we can do as individuals or as a church to reduce our carbon footprints. It goes right to the heart of our faith and spiritual calling and challenges us to be a prophetic voice for climate justice.

(Operationnoah.org)

Some of the other ways that Christian churches and individual Christians can support the work of Operation Noah are through:

- encouraging their local church community to become more involved in environmental issues, such as asking them not to use companies that rely on fossil-fuels
- taking part in 'Pray and Fast for the Climate'. This is an initiative where Christians 'pray and fast' on the first of each month (either on their own or with others) in the hope that God will use their prayers to influence the politicians who make environmental decisions, make their campaigning successful and inspire others to take action
- lobbying local politicians and MPs
- speaking out or writing articles on environmental issues such as pollution, global warming and limiting the use of natural resources
- fundraising or donating money.

Christian responses to animal rights

In the past, Christianity has been criticised for its attitude towards animals, which has led to animals being seen purely as a resource for human beings to use as they wish. Today, the vast majority of Christians would agree that animals are an important part of God's creation. However, they have different views about the role of animals and how they should be treated. Most Christians do not think that animals have the same rights as human

Figure 4.11 Cecil the lion, when he was alive. Many Christians condemned his killing and used it to highlight how we mistreat animals

Sources of authority

The righteous care for the needs of their animals,… (Proverbs, 12:10)

Sources of authority

'We do not own the world, and its riches are not ours to dispose of at will. Show a loving consideration for all creatures, and seek to maintain the beauty and variety of the world. Work to ensure that our increasing power over nature is used responsibly, with reverence for life.'

(Quaker Faith and Practice, 42, Chapter 1)

Sources of authority

Animals are God's creatures, not human property, nor utilities, nor resources, nor commodities, but precious beings in God's sight. …Christians whose eyes are fixed on the awfulness of crucifixion are in a special position to understand the awfulness of innocent suffering. The Cross of Christ is God's absolute identification with the weak, the powerless, and the vulnerable, but most of all with unprotected, undefended, innocent suffering.

(Andrew Linzey on vegetarianism, 2005)

Sources of authority

Then he asked them, 'If one of you has a child or an ox that falls into a well on the Sabbath day, will you not immediately pull it out?' (Luke, 14:5)

beings. Nevertheless, they still think that they should be treated in a humane and compassionate way as this shows responsible stewardship of the Earth instead of domination of the Earth.

Many Christians disagree with 'blood sports', intensive farming methods, vivisection, which means using animals for scientific experimentation and animal testing in connection with toiletries and cosmetics. Others also disagree with circuses that use animals, zoos, fur coats and eating meat. Some Christians, however, accept that using animals for food, to test the safety of medicines and chemicals and to improve veterinary knowledge is acceptable; providing all of the methods are subject to good animal husbandry and meet ethical and animal welfare guidelines.

The Religious Society of Friends (Quakers) is a Christian denomination that have always been very concerned about the rights of animals.

Professor Andrew Linzey, a British Anglican priest, is regarded as a leading authority on Christianity and animals. He has been preaching and writing about animal rights since the 1970s and is an important figure in the Christian vegetarian movement. Linzey is also on the board of The Christian Vegetarian Association and is the founder of the Oxford Centre for Animal Ethics. He argues that animals have special moral claim on human beings because they are so innocent. They are unable to speak out for themselves, which makes them vulnerable to exploitation by humans. According to Linzey, this means that inflicting suffering on them is very hard to justify.

Some Christians might argue that being a vegetarian is more spiritual and more compatible with a modern understanding of Christian stewardship. Many Christians, however, are not vegetarian as they do not believe that this is what God requires of them. They might argue that the Bible supports the eating of meat and it does not mean that they are not good stewards of the Earth if they eat it. Increasing numbers of Christians are becoming concerned about animal welfare standards in the food industry. Some might only eat meat if they can be assured that the animal has not been intensively farmed but has been treated well and been able to roam freely until it has been killed for food.

Sources of authority

About noon the following day as they were on their journey and approaching the city, Peter went up on the roof to pray. He became hungry and wanted something to eat, and while the meal was being prepared, he fell into a trance. He saw heaven opened and something like a large sheet being let down to earth by its four corners. It contained all kinds of four-footed animals, as well as reptiles and birds. Then a voice told him, 'Get up, Peter. Kill and eat.' (Acts, 10:9–13)

Anglican Society for the Welfare of Animals

The Anglican Society for the Welfare of Animals (ASWA) is a Church of England Organisation that was founded to draw the attention of Christians and non-Christians alike to the abuse of animals and to make them aware of the importance of caring for all of creation. They believe that intensive farming (including fur farming), vivisection, mistreatment of pets and the killing of animals for pleasure raises serious ethical questions and should be on the agenda of every church.

The ASWA encourages churches and individuals to include animal welfare concerns in their prayers and to hold animal blessing services. Through education and lawful action and working with other organisations who share their objectives they aim to improve the conservation of animals and their welfare. It believes that the Bible teaches everyone that they should care for animals and rescue those in distress.

Activities ?

1   Design a symbol to represent the Christian understanding of stewardship today and explain your design.
2   Role-play, with a partner, two Christians discussing their different attitudes towards animals. Summarise your discussion afterwards.
3   Prepare a three-minute presentation for the rest of your class on an environmental or animal rights issue that concerns you and what you think could be done to change it.

Can you remember?

- What are the differences between passive and active euthanasia and why might people agree with one of these but not the other?
- Why do most Christians disagree with euthanasia?
- What are the key arguments that atheists and Humanists put forward in support of euthanasia?

Exam-style question

'The natural world must be protected'. Evaluate this statement considering arguments for and against what it says.

In your response you should:
- refer to Christian teachings
- refer to non-religious points of view
- reach a justified conclusion. **(12 marks)**

Exam tip

Make sure that you know and can explain Christian responses to environmental and animal rights issues.

Summary

- Christians believe that stewardship is a way of life. This means they have a responsibility to try to protect and improve the environment. Operation Noah is an ecumenical Christian charity which is very concerned about climate change. It says that the time has now come for everyone, particularly Christians, to take action against this.
- In the past, Christianity has been criticised for its attitude towards animals. Today most Christians believe that animals are an important part of God's creation. However, they have different ideas about the role of animals and, in some cases, how they should be treated. The Anglican Society for the Welfare of Animals (ASWA) is a Church of England Organisation, which aims to educate people about the importance of caring for all of creation. It also campaigns to stop the abuse of animals.

Checkpoint

Strengthen

S1 Why do Christians believe that they have a responsibility to protect the environment?

S2 What are Shrinking the Footprint and Operation Noah?

S3 How do Christians support animal rights?

Challenge

C1 What do Christians mean when they say that stewardship is a way of life?

C2 Why might some Christians think that the Church should not get involved in politics?

C3 How could vegetarianism be seen as a more spiritual option from a Christian perspective?

Recap: Matters of life and death

The activities on these two pages will help you to remember the things you have learnt in this chapter. It is important that you consolidate your knowledge about 'Matters of life and death' as this will help you to make connections between the topics from each of the previous chapters:

- Christian beliefs
- Living the Christian life
- Marriage and the family.

Recall quiz

The origins and value of the universes

1 How did Georges Lemaitre explain the origins of the universe?
2 What does Christianity teach about the value of the universe?
3 Why has Christianity been criticised for its attitude towards the universe?

Sanctity of life

4 What does the term sanctity of life mean?
5 What is the significance of a belief in the sanctity of life for Christians today?

The origins and value of human life

6 How does Science explain the origins of human life?
7 Why do Christians believe that human life is of value?
8 What do atheists and Humanists think about the value of human life?

Abortion

9 What does Christianity teach about abortion?
10 How do different Christians respond to the issue of abortion?

Death and the afterlife

11 Why do Christians believe in the afterlife?
12 What other reasons do some people have for believing in an afterlife?
13 Why do atheists and Humanists reject a belief in the afterlife?

Euthanasia

14 What implications does euthanasia have for the value and sanctity of human life from a Christian perspective?
15 Why do some people want euthanasia to be legalised?
16 What is hospice care?

Christian responses to issues in the natural world

17 How do Christians respond to the issue of animal rights?
18 What do Christians believe to be the responsibilities of stewardship in today's world?'

Exam tips

- Make sure that you understand and can explain atheist and Humanist views on the value of the human person.
- Make sure you can understand and can explain non-religious arguments against an afterlife.
- Ensure that you understand and can explain scientific theories about the origins of the universe and human beings and the different Christian responses to them.
- Make sure you understand and can explain different Christian beliefs and non-religious views about abortion. Remember to refer back to the quote when answering the question.
- Make sure you understand and can explain different Christian beliefs and non-religious views about life after death. Remember to refer back to the quote when answering the question.
- Ensure that you can support your statements with a source of wisdom and authority.

Exam-style questions

(a) Explain two reasons why atheists and Humanists believe that human life is of value. **(4 marks)**

(b) Outline three reasons why Christians reject non-religious arguments against an afterlife. **(3 marks)**

(c) Explain two Christian responses to scientific theories about the origins of the universe and human beings. You must refer to a source of wisdom and authority in your answer. **(5 marks)**

(d) 'We must not be surprised when we hear of murders, killings, of wars, or of hatred… If a mother can kill her own child, what is left but for us to kill each other?' Mother Teresa

Evaluate this statement considering arguments for and against what it says. In your response you should:

- refer to Christian teachings. • refer to non-religious points of view • reach a justified conclusion. **(12 marks)**

In the following question, 3 of the marks awarded will be for your spelling, punctuation and grammar and your use of specialist terminology.

(e) 'An astronomically overwhelming majority of the people who could be born never will be. You are one of the tiny minority whose number came up. Be thankful that you have a life, and forsake your vain and presumptuous desire for a second one.' Richard Dawkin

Evaluate this statement considering arguments for and against what it says. In your response you should:

- refer to Christian teachings • refer to non-religious points of view • reach a justified conclusion. **(15 marks)**

Activities

1 Produce a glossary of all the key terms in this chapter. An alternative task could be to explain what each topic is about or summarise each topic in this chapter using no more than three sentences or identify what you think are the two most important keywords/phrases for each topic and say why you have chosen them.

2 Imagine that you are a Christian. Discuss with a partner how might you respond to the ultimate questions that were raised in the introduction to this topic:
- Where does life come from? • What is the purpose of life? • What happens when we die?
- Why do we exist? • When does life begin?

3 Use the information in the Summary of learning for each topic in this chapter to prepare revision materials. This could take the form of revision cards for each topic in this chapter or a concept map which notes the key ideas and learning points. Remember to:
- use and highlight the key terms, making sure that you know what they mean
- include relevant biblical references.

4 Many people who agree with euthanasia say that the quality of a person's life is really important consideration. In groups, discuss and make a list of the things you think people need to have a good quality of life or make their life worthwhile, apart from food, water and shelter.

5 Conduct a class survey to find out the attitudes towards abortion and euthanasia. Summarise your research and suggest reasons for your findings.

Summary of learning:

In this chapter you have learned about different Christian beliefs on matters of life and death and their responses to these issues:
- scientific explanations for the origins of the universe and the value of the universe
- the sanctity of life
- non-religious explanations for the origins and value of human life
- abortion
- death and the afterlife
- euthanasia
- the natural world, including animal rights.

You will have also learned what atheists and Humanists think about some of these issues.

Extend: Matters of life and death

The Assisted Dying Bill was debated by MPs on Friday 11 September 2015. After four hours of passionate debate the Bill was voted down by a large majority of MPs. The purpose of the Assisted Dying Bill was to legalise voluntary euthanasia by enabling 'competent adults who are terminally ill to be provided at their request with specified assistance to end their own life; and for connected purposes'.

Reading Sources 1 and 2 and doing the activities below, together with the other things you have learned in this chapter, will help you to answer the exam question at the end of this section.

Source 1

UK parliament votes heavily against assisted suicide

John McDermott and Sarah Neville

Members of parliament on Friday voted against a bill to allow people with terminal illnesses to end their lives with medical supervision, after an emotionally fraught and philosophical debate in the House of Commons that reflected the deep differences of opinion among British people.

The private member's bill put forward by Rob Marris, Labour MP from Wolverhampton, was defeated, with 118 MPs in favour and 330 against his plans to allow 'competent' adults with fewer than six months to live to seek professional help to kill themselves.

The size of the majority is a setback for campaigners who want England and Wales to follow the Benelux countries and Switzerland, as well as US states such as Oregon, in legalising assisted suicide.

One MP described it as a 'once in generation defeat'.

Opening the debate on Friday, Natascha Engel, deputy speaker of the House said that she had received 'unprecedented' requests from MPs to speak. [...]

Speaking in support of the bill, Sarah Champion, a Labour MP, said that 'this house does not have a moral superiority' over those making their own decisions about their deaths.

Others spoke of their religious convictions. Opposing the bill, Caroline Spelman said 'life is a gift from God with all the pain and suffering that it entails'.

Ms Spelman's colleague, Sir Edward Leigh, agreed, asking 'what kind of society do we want to create?' when legislation supports the extinguishing of an 'eternal soul'.

Fellow Conservative Crispin Blunt, however, disagreed. Turning to colleagues around him, the MP implored that 'we are the party of freedom and choice'.

Liam Fox, Conservative MP and a doctor, said the bill would have 'opened a Pandora's box' and risked 'fundamentally changing the relationship between doctor and patients'.

The medical profession remains divided over the merits of assisted suicide but the British Medical Association has been formally opposed to making it legal to help hasten patients' deaths for almost a decade. Faith leaders, including the Archbishop of Canterbury, Justin Welby, united to argue against the measure.

Jacky Davis, a consultant radiologist from north London, who chairs Health Professionals for Assisted Dying, said the bill's defeat left her feeling 'a bit flat having worked so hard for it' but added that the issue 'is not going to go away'.

Sarah Wootton, chief executive of Dignity in Dying, added that the vote 'only goes to show just how ridiculously out of touch MPs are with the British public on the issue'. She claimed an 'overwhelming majority' supported the bill. Opinion polls suggest most Britons favour a change in the law, though the level of support depends on the wording of the pollsters' question.

Mark Atkinson, interim chief executive at disability charity Scope, said disabled people would be 'extremely relieved' that the legislation had been so convincingly defeated.

'Keeping the current law means giving crucial protection to the lives of disabled and other vulnerable people, who could feel they are a burden to society', he added.

In 2010, Keir Starmer MP, then the Director of Public Prosecutions, said that family or friends who travelled with a loved one to the Swiss suicide group Dignitas would not risk prosecution — but medical professionals have not been offered such protections. [...]

(extracted text) Copyright The Financial Times 2016

Source 2

More views on assisted dying

Prior to the vote the Archbishop of Canterbury, Justin Welby, (the main leader of the Church of England) together with other faith leaders, issued a joint letter urging MPs to reject the bill. Their view is that the bill went beyond 'merely legitimising suicide to actively supporting it'. Writing in The Observer newspaper, the archbishop maintained that 'respect for the lives of others goes to the heart of both our criminal and human rights laws and ought not to be abandoned'.

However, TheTelegraph reported that a previous Archbishop of Canterbury, George Carey is supportive of assisted dying. He believes that doctors helping terminally ill people to die would be 'profoundly moral and Christian thing to do' as there is nothing 'noble' about enduring severe pain.

The Royal College of Nursing has a neutral stance in relation to assisted dying.

Activities   ?

1   Read Source 1 and answer the questions below.

   a   What was the Assisted Dying Bill and what was its key proposal to change the existing law?

   b   How did MPs respond to the Assisted Dying Bill when it was presented to parliament?

   c   What various arguments in support of the Assisted Dying Bill were used by: Sarah Champion MP, Sarah
       Wootton (Dignity in Dying), Crispin Blunt MP and George Carey, the former Archbishop of Canterbury?

   d   What various arguments against the Assisted Dying Bill were used by Caroline Spelman, Sir Edward Leigh,
       Liam Fox MP, the BMA, Justin Welby, Mark Atkinson of Scope and Kier Starmer MP?

   e   Give reasons why you think a terminally ill person might want to choose when and how to die.

   f   Explain why some people may be worried about the lack of protection for the vulnerable if euthanasia or
       assisted dying was legalised and why they might think that a disabled or terminally ill person might feel
       pressure to end their life through assisted dying if the law was changed.

   g   Summarise why the medical profession might feel concerned about a change in law regarding euthanasia.

   h   Why were MPs accused of being out of date?

   i   How do the ideas in the Assisted Dying Bill conflict with the Christian belief in the sanctity of life?

2   Review Topics 4.2 and 4.4. Summarise how the issues of abortion, euthanasia and the sanctity of life are
    connected. Explain why you think it might be that some Christians could be pro-choice for abortion but totally
    opposed to euthanasia.

Exam-style question

'A right to die could quickly become a duty to die.'

Evaluate this statement considering arguments for
and against what it says. In your response you should:

- refer to Christian teachings
- refer to non-religious points of view
- reach a justified conclusion.

(12 marks)

Exam tips

- Ensure you know the different types of euthanasia.
- Make sure that you understand and can explain
  a range of different arguments for and against
  euthanasia, including Christian, atheist and
  Humanist views.
- Ensure that you can support Christian views with a
  source of wisdom and authority.
- Ensure that you have considered the possible
  impact on society if euthanasia were to become
  legalised in the UK.
- Make sure that you have thought about and
  formulated your own views on euthanasia.
- Always try to plan your arguments when debating an
  issue so that you put forward a balanced response.
- Use connectives to give your arguments a logical
  structure and make the contrasts clear.
- Make sure that the language you use is measured
  and accurately represents the views you are trying
  to express.
- Always draw together what you have written in a
  conclusion to finish the debate or discussion.

Preparing for your Christianity Paper 1 exam

In specification B, the exam has three papers covering three areas of study, from which you choose two. The papers are:

- Paper 1: Religion and ethics
- Paper 2: Religion, peace and conflict
- Paper 3: Religion, philosophy and social justice

The exam for Paper 1 on Religion and ethics will last for 1 hour and 45 minutes (105 minutes). It will count for 50% of the GCSE qualification. In your exam you will be asked to respond to questions which relate to the topics you have studied in this book. These are listed below.

The remaining 50% of the GCSE qualification will come from the study of a different religion. You will be examined, for example, on Islam in either Paper 2 or Paper 3, depending on the topics that have been chosen by your school. The topics for Islam Paper 2 and Paper 3 are listed on page 142, demonstrating the overall topic structure that is echoed across each of the religions available to study.

Christianity Paper 1: Religion and ethics

Christian beliefs

- ☐ The nature of God
  - beliefs about God
  - the doctrine of the Trinity
- ☐ Creation
  - Christian beliefs
  - significance for Christians today
- ☐ The Incarnation
  - Jesus as the incarnate son of God
  - significance for Christians today
- ☐ The last days of Jesus' life
  - the events of Jesus' last days on earth
  - how these help Christians to understand the meaning and purpose of Jesus' time on earth
- ☐ Atonement and salvation
  - teachings and significance
  - beliefs about Jesus' role in atonement and salvation
- ☐ Eschatology: life after death
  - beliefs, especially relating to life after death
  - evil and suffering
  - reconciling belief in God with a world where there is evil
  - beliefs about evil and suffering

Living the Christian life

- ☐ Christian worship
  - why worship is important for Christians
  - private and communal worship
  - liturgical and non-liturgical worship
- ☐ The role of the sacraments
  - their meaning
  - their role in Christian life
  - how they are celebrated
- ☐ The nature and purpose of prayer
  - what prayer is
  - why Christians pray
  - different types of prayer
  - when/where/why they are used
- ☐ Pilgrimage
  - its nature, history and purpose
  - the significance of major pilgrimage sites
  - its importance today
- ☐ Christian religious celebrations
  - Christmas
  - Easter
- ☐ The local parish Church
  - its role in the community
  - its importance in the community

☐ The worldwide Church and its future
- its role and importance
- its teachings on charity and support for the worldwide community
- its work for reconciliation
- missionary and evangelical work

Marriage and the family

☐ Marriage
- the purpose of marriage and its significance in society
- atheist and Humanist attitudes to marriage and cohabitation
- Christian attitudes to cohabitation

☐ Sexual relationships
- the Christian view
- atheist and Humanist views

☐ Families
- different types of family
- their importance and purpose
- atheist and Humanist views

☐ Support for the family in the local parish
- why local churches try to support families
- the importance of such support

☐ Contraception
- different Christian views
- atheist and Humanist views

☐ Divorce
- different Christian views
- atheist and Humanist views

☐ Equality of men and women in the family
- different Christian views
- atheist and Humanist views

☐ Gender prejudice and discrimination
- meaning
- Christian opposition
- atheist and Humanist views

Matters of life and death

☐ The origins and value of the universe
- scientific theories and Christian responses to them
- the value of the universe in Christian teaching
- Christian responses to the universe as a commodity

☐ The sanctity of life
- Christian beliefs about the sanctity of life
- its importance for Christians today

☐ The origins and value of human life
- scientific and non-religious views and their significance for Christians

☐ Abortion
- the nature of abortion
- Christian teachings on abortion
- atheist and Humanist views and Christian responses to them

☐ Death and the afterlife
- Christian teachings on the afterlife
- atheist, Humanist and other views
- why Christians uphold a belief in the afterlife

☐ Euthanasia
- Christian teachings and beliefs
- atheist and Humanist views and Christian responses to them

☐ Christian support for hospice care as an alternative to euthanasia
- Christian responses to issues in the natural world
- beliefs about stewardship
- responses to environmental issues
- responses to animal-rights issues

Preparing for your exam

Choose **either** Paper 2 **or** Paper 3 in your second religion, for example Islam.

Islam Paper 2: Religion, peace and conflict

Muslim beliefs
- [ ] The six beliefs of Islam
- [ ] The five roots of Usul'al din in Shia Islam
- [ ] The nature of Allah
- [ ] Risalah: prophethood
- [ ] Muslim holy books (kutub)
- [ ] Malaikah: angels
- [ ] Al Qadr: predestination
- [ ] Akhirah: life after death

Crime and punishment
- [ ] Justice
- [ ] Causes of crime
- [ ] Good, evil and suffering
- [ ] Punishment
- [ ] Aims of punishment
- [ ] Forgiveness
- [ ] The treatment of criminals
- [ ] Capital punishment

Living the Muslim life
- [ ] Ten Obligatory Acts of Shi'a Islam
- [ ] Shahadah: the declaration of faith
- [ ] Salah: prayer
- [ ] Sawm: fasting
- [ ] Zakah and Khums: the giving of alms
- [ ] Hajj: pilgrimage to Mecca
- [ ] Jihad
- [ ] Celebration and commemoration

Peace and conflict
- [ ] Peace
- [ ] Peacemaking
- [ ] Conflict
- [ ] Pacifism and passive resistance
- [ ] Just War
- [ ] Holy War
- [ ] Weapons of mass destruction
- [ ] The issues of conflict

Islam Paper 3: Religion, philosophy and social justice

Muslim beliefs
- [ ] The six beliefs of Islam
- [ ] The five roots of Usul'al din in Shia Islam
- [ ] The nature of Allah
- [ ] Risalah: prophethood
- [ ] Muslim holy books (kutub)
- [ ] Malaikah: angels
- [ ] Al Qadr: predestination
- [ ] Akhirah: life after death

Religious beliefs
- [ ] Revelation
- [ ] Visions
- [ ] Miracles
- [ ] The design argument
- [ ] The cosmological argument
- [ ] Issues raised by the existence of suffering
- [ ] Practical and philosophical solutions offered to the problem of suffering

Living the Muslim life
- [ ] Ten Obligatory Acts of Shi'a Islam
- [ ] Shahadah: the declaration of faith
- [ ] Salah: prayer
- [ ] Sawm: fasting
- [ ] Zakah and Khums: the giving of alms
- [ ] Hajj: pilgrimage to Mecca
- [ ] Jihad
- [ ] Celebration and commemoration

Equality
- [ ] Human rights
- [ ] Equality
- [ ] Religious freedom
- [ ] Prejudice and discrimination
- [ ] Racial harmony
- [ ] Racial discrimination
- [ ] Social justice
- [ ] Wealth and poverty

The questions

In the exam for Paper 1 you will be asked to answer four questions in writing. These will be on each of the chapters you have studied:

- Christian beliefs
- Living the Christian life
- Marriage and the family
- Matters of life and death.

Each of the four questions, numbered 1 to 4, will be in parts: a), b), c) and d). All of the parts carry different marks. You must answer all parts of a question in order to gain the most marks.

The following is an example of a *complete* exam question based on Chapter 2, Living the Christian life:

1 a) Outline three features of baptism.   (3 marks)

   b) Explain two reasons why Christians might have different attitudes towards prayer.   (4 marks)

   c) Explain two reasons why the festival of Christmas is significant for Christians. In your answer you must refer to a source of wisdom and authority.   (5 marks)

   d) 'Christians are right to proselytise.' Evaluate this statement, considering arguments for and against what it is saying. In your response you should:
   refer to Christian teachings
   refer to different Christian points of view
   reach a justified conclusion.   (12 marks)

   Total = 24 marks

Exam tip

Remember that you must try to answer all parts (a–d) of each of the four questions.

Question types

The paper is likely to include a combination of short open response, long open response and extended writing questions.

Typically, part a) and b) questions will ask you to outline or explain something. These are examples of short open response questions.

Open response (part c), and extended writing questions (part d), will carry the most marks. This is because you are expected to provide more detailed responses. You should also include a reference to a source of wisdom and authority, such as a quote from the Bible, in answers to part c) and often part d) questions.

In **open response questions** you can choose what information to include, depending on which points you think are most relevant to the question.

Extended writing questions are also open response questions but they are a longer and more developed piece of writing which discusses issues in more depth and comes to a conclusion.

Mark scheme

- You will be awarded up to 3 marks for a correct answer to part a) questions.
- You will be awarded up to 4 marks for a correct answer to part b) questions.
- You will be awarded up to 5 marks for a correct answer to part c) questions.
- You will be awarded up to 12 marks for a correct answer to part d) questions.

In two out of the four part d) questions you will be awarded up to 3 additional marks for your spelling, punctuation, grammar (SPaG) and your use of specialist terminology. This means that some part d) questions will be worth a maximum of 15 marks.

'Specialist terminology' means the specific key words and phrases associated with the issue that the question is focused on. For example, *annulment* is an example of specialist terminology that you might use when discussing the issue of divorce. Specialist terminology is highlighted in bold for you throughout the book, and definitions are given in the glossary on pages 154–159.

Preparing for your exam

Paper 2 is worth a total of 102 marks. The breakdown of marks across the four complete questions, including marks for SPaG and use of specialist terminology, is as follows:

- Question 1 is worth a maximum of 27 marks
- Question 2 is worth a maximum of 24 marks
- Question 3 is worth a maximum of 27 marks
- Question 4 is worth a maximum of 24 marks.

Examiners will mark your answers according to a mark scheme. The mark scheme has two assessment objectives: AO1 and AO2.

Assessment Objective 1

Assessment objective 1 (AO1) focuses on your ability to demonstrate your knowledge and understanding of Christianity. This means that an examiner will be reading what you have written and assessing what you know about:

- Christian beliefs, practices and sources of authority, e.g. what Christians believe, what they base those beliefs on, and what attitudes they have and how they act as a result of those beliefs.
- the influence of Christian beliefs on individuals, communities and societies, e.g. the impact that Christian beliefs have on the lives of individual Christians, their local communities and the world.
- the similarities and differences within and/or between individual Christians and Christian groups, e.g. the way individual Christians or denominations can believe and practise different things, even though they are all part of the same religion.

Assessment Objective 2

Assessment Objective 2 (AO2) focuses on your ability to analyse and evaluate aspects of Christianity and Christian beliefs. You will need to show that you can communicate different points of view using reasons and evidence, on topics including:

- the influence and significance of Christianity and Christian beliefs, e.g. the importance of Christianity and Christian beliefs and the meaning and impact that they might have on the lives of individual Christians, the Christian community and the wider society in which the Christian community exists
- your ability to make connections between different aspects of Christian beliefs
- your ability to use evidence from what you have learned to reach a justified conclusion in the part d) questions.

Revision strategy

The key to success in exams often lies in good planning. Make sure you know what you need to do and when you need to do it. **Start early by making the most of your lessons!** The more you understand, learn and practise as you go along, the less intensive revision you will need to do.

Try to make sure that you always understand everything you have been taught. Most importantly, ask for help or clarification if you need it. Take every opportunity to put your learning into practice throughout the GCSE course by doing the activities and practice exam-style questions in this book. Taking part in class discussions is also an excellent way of developing your learning.

Planning your revision time

Make sure you know what revision strategies work best for you in this subject. It is also important that you are realistic about how much time you have for revision and how much you can fit into one revision session. Planning a revision timetable well in advance of your exams can help with this.

Exam tip

Breaking up your revision into smaller chunks will make it more manageable.

Everyone is different, but 'a little and often' is thought to be the best way to tackle revision – perhaps revising one or two connected topics at a time. A thorough programme of revision is essential if you are to do well in your exams.

Know your strengths

Analyse your strengths and the areas you need to develop using your own insights and the feedback you get from your class teacher throughout the course. Try to address any gaps in your knowledge and understanding straight away. Don't avoid it, because not understanding or knowing something now could make it harder to learn other things later.

Exam tip

Remember to review your progress regularly as you work through the course. This will let you see where you have improved and what you still need to work on.

As you finish each topic, make a list of how well you know it. You can use the checklist on pages 140–141 to help. Try to identify areas that you know less about or don't understand, and use the book or ask your teacher or one of your classmates to help you improve. Don't forget to celebrate your strengths. These are a good foundation on which to build and will help you to further develop your knowledge and understanding.

Most importantly, have confidence in your ability to do well!

Get Connected!

The other important thing to do is to try to **make connections between the things you have learned**. This will make the information much easier to remember and help you to revise more efficiently. The diagram below shows the way in which different aspects of Christianity can be connected.

Making connections is easy! Start with a key Christian belief about God and get connected.

What connections can you make between things that you have learned?

In groups, each pick a different belief about God or Jesus from Chapter 1 and draw a 'get connected' diagram to share with the group. Use the chapter and topic summary at the beginning of this section or the more detailed checklist at the end of the book to help you.

A Christian belief in the Trinity is connected to the belief that God, as the Father, created the universe.

The Christian belief that God created the universe demonstrates that God is all-powerful and has control over everything that exists. This belief is connected to the problem of evil and suffering and the nature of God.

It is also connected to belief that all life is sacred and has value because it has been created by God, in the image of God. This is known as the sanctity of life. The Christian belief in the sanctity of life is connected to Christian attitudes and beliefs about matters of life and death, such as abortion and euthanasia. There are other connections too between a belief in the sanctity and value of human life and campaigning against gender prejudice and discrimination and doing charitable work.

Another connection can be made between Christian beliefs about the creation of the universe and Christian attitudes towards the natural world, i.e. stewardship.

Understanding the question

It is important that you understand exactly what it is that you are being asked to do when answering a question. Read every question carefully at least twice. Pay attention to the number of marks and the command words. As mentioned previously, the number of marks gives you an idea of how many minutes you should spend answering the question.

Command words

Each question will contain a command word. Command words are important because they tell you how you should respond to the question, as in what the examiner is asking you to do. The command words that you are likely to find in the exam paper are:

- Outline
- State
- Describe
- Explain
- Evaluate

Unpicking the question

In addition to command words, questions will also contain other information that can help you to answer the question correctly. For example, in the following questions, useful words that tell you what to write about have been underlined.

c) '**Explain** two ways Christians seek to <u>defend their belief</u> in an all-loving God in the face of <u>evil and suffering</u> in the world.
In your answer you must refer to a source of wisdom and authority. (5 marks)

d) 'The aim of all humans is to achieve salvation and go to heaven when they die.' **Evaluate** this statement, considering it from <u>more than one perspective</u>.
In your response you should:
– refer to Christian teachings
– refer to different Christian points of view
– reach a justified conclusion. (12 marks)

> **Exam tips**
>
> Question c) is asking you to give details about Christian beliefs about the nature or qualities of God (what Christians believe God is like) and how this fits with evil and suffering. You need to show that you understand the difficulties some Christians might have in explaining the presence of evil and suffering, if God is meant to be loving and good, together with some of the ideas that have been put forward by Christians to explain how evil and suffering can exist without it being God's fault.

> **Exam tips**
>
> Question d) is asking you to discuss and weigh up (evaluate) whether or not this statement is true from at least two different viewpoints, one of which must be a Christian perspective. You would need to write about the Christian idea of salvation (what it means and involves) and heaven. It is also asking you to discuss whether it is the aim of all humans (religious and non-religious) to achieve this, giving examples of non-religious views (such as atheist or Humanist) or other non-Christian religious beliefs to support your arguments. Lastly, a conclusion is needed, summarising your evaluation of the issue.

Answering the question

With a good plan, you should be able to answer the question with no problems. Below are examples of answers to exam-style questions. The questions have been unpicked for you and the command words are highlighted.

Plan your answer

It's a good idea to plan your answer before you start writing it. Once you have understood what the question is asking, take a minute to think about how you want to respond. Ask yourself:

- What is the question asking me to do: outline, state, describe, explain or evaluate?
- What does the wording of the question say it is about?
- What key points do I need to make?
- How many points do I need to make?
- How many points do I need to make and develop?
- What specialist terminology should I use?
- Do I need to include more than one point of view?
- Will I need to put forward arguments and provide evidence to support them?
- Do I need a conclusion?

Keep focused

Make sure you know what you are going to say before you start writing. Have a plan for the structure and content of your response. Take a minute to write down a few bullet points or words about the information you are going to put in your answer, covering the order in which you are going to write your points and the specialist terminology you need to include. Try to tick off each point as you go, particularly for questions that require a longer answer. This will help you to stay focused on the question and not write about something irrelevant. You have enough time in the exam to answer each question correctly, provided you don't stray off the point.

Check your answer

Always try to read back through everything you have written to check that it makes sense and says what you wanted it to. The examiner will award you marks on the basis of what you have actually written, not what you meant to write.

Make sure your handwriting is clear and easy to read. It does not need to be perfect, but the examiner must be able to read it! They will not be able to give you marks for something they cannot read properly. Poor handwriting can also affect the clarity of what you are trying to say in your responses.

Activities ?

1. Pick an answer that you wrote to one of the questions in the first chapter of the book. Review it against the example answers and list three things that you could improve about it.

2. In pairs or small groups, choose a part d) exam-style question from the book and create a plan for how to answer it. Think about how you want to structure your response as well as what you want to say.

3. Swap an answer that you've written previously with someone else in your class. Give each other helpful ideas about how they could make it better, or what you might have done differently. Then compare your answers.

Christianity Paper 1, part a)

a) Outline three Christian beliefs about the creation of the world.

(3 marks)

Exam tips

- Always use capital letters to begin sentences and for proper nouns (names), including 'God' or 'Allah'.
- Do not write in capitals. Use the correct combination of capitals and lower-case letters throughout your work.
- Remember that, even within a religion, not everyone believes exactly the same things.

Sample answer 1

Christians believe that God created the world and they also believe that the creation is good. All Christians believe that the world was created in six days as it says in the Bible.

Verdict – needs developing

- A question that asks you to *outline* something is asking you to recall factual information you have learned. Questions like this are usually worth 3 marks. You will normally be expected to make three separate points and can be awarded 1 mark for each correct point you make.
- This answer correctly identifies two Christian beliefs about creation: that it was the work of God and that it is good.
- However, it is an error to say that all Christians believe the world was created in six days. Some Christians accept the biblical account literally, but many understand it to be a metaphor.

Sample answer 2

Christians believe that the universe and everything in it was created by God who is all-powerful. They also believe, as they are taught in Genesis, that God looked on his creation and found it was good. Christians believe that human beings are created in the image and likeness of God.

Verdict – strong

- This answer provides three Christian beliefs about creation.
- Each of these beliefs is taught in the Bible and they are held by all mainstream Christians.

christianity Paper 1, part b)

b) Explain two Christian beliefs about the Incarnation of Jesus. **(4 marks)**

Exam tips

- The way you present you work in examinations is important. Write clearly and try to avoid crossings out.
- Always write in full sentences. Do not use text-messaging or online chat abbreviations.

Sample answer 1

Incarnation means 'becoming flesh'. The Incarnation means that Jesus was God. For this reason Christians see Jesus as more than a teacher, but worship him as divine.

Verdict – needs developing

- A question that asks you to *explain* something is asking you to demonstrate your knowledge of a particular aspect of Christianity by recalling factual information you have learned and developing it. Questions like this are usually worth 4 marks. You will normally be expected to make and develop two separate points. A maximum of 2 marks can be awarded for each separate point.
- This answer correctly identifies one Christian belief about the Incarnation.
- The belief is also developed by drawing out one significance of that belief.
- However, the first reason, that incarnation means becoming flesh, only explains the meaning of the term. It does not explain the term as a Christian belief and there is no development.

Sample answer 2

The Incarnation is important to Christians because it teaches that Jesus was both God and human. For this reason, Christians respect Jesus as more than a teacher; they also worship him as divine. When Jesus became human he was able to understand and share difficult human experiences. An example of this is when, in the Garden of Gethsemane, his human nature shared the human fear of pain, namely his coming crucifixion.

Verdict – strong

- This answer correctly identifies two Christian reasons why the Incarnation of Jesus is important for Christians.
- Both reasons are developed, one by drawing out the significance of the belief and the other by giving an example of the importance of Jesus' human nature in his own life.
- The developments relate both to the reasons given and to the question.

Explaining why something is important requires more than defining the meaning of a word or phrase.

Christianity Paper 1, part c)

c) Explain two reasons why belief in life after death is important for Christians.
In your answer you must refer to a source of wisdom and authority.

(5 marks)

Exam tips

- What you choose to leave out of a question can be just as important as what you decide to include. Choose arguments that you know you can support with evidence.

- Use paragraphs to help structure your work. You should have a new paragraph for every key idea or point that you are making and developing.

Sample answer 1

Belief in life after death is what gives human life meaning and purpose. St Paul taught in his letter to the Romans that death cannot separate people from the love of Christ.

Verdict – needs developing

- This answer explains one reason why life after death is important for Christians.
- It provides one source of wisdom and authority (St Paul's letter to the Romans) on the subject of why Christians are confident in their belief in life after death.
- However, it is not clear how the source of wisdom and authority helps to explain why belief in life after death is important to Christians.
- Also, two reasons are needed and they both need to be developed.

Sample answer 2

For Christians, belief in life after death gives human life meaning and purpose. Because they have the ultimate goal of eternal life with God, they devote their lives to living in accordance with God's will. Belief in life after death is also important for Christians because it explains the purpose of the death and resurrection of Jesus. By Jesus dying to save sinful humanity, and rising again, everyone is able to live in hope of going to heaven. St Paul taught in his letter to the Romans that death cannot separate people from the love of Christ.

Verdict – strong

- There are two developed reasons for why belief in life after death is important to Christians.
- There is reference to a source of wisdom and authority.
- The source relates directly to a reason why the belief is important.

The source of wisdom and authority needs to relate directly to the question.

Christianity Paper 1, part d)

In this question, 3 of the marks awarded will be for your spelling, punctuation and grammar and your use of specialist terminology.

d) 'Jesus died so that everyone can go to heaven.'
  • Evaluate this statement, considering arguments for and against.
  • In your response you should:
  • refer to Christian teachings
  • refer to different Christian points of view
  • reach a justified conclusion.

(15 marks)

Exam tips

• Construct your sentences well. Make sure they are not too long. Use commas, colons and semicolons where appropriate and finish all of your sentences with a full stop.

• In extended answer questions, make sure you always express your own views in a balanced and measured way. Ensure you link your views to the statement and other ideas that you have written about.

Sample answer 1

Christians believe that Jesus died to bring salvation to a sinful world. This is known as the atonement. Because Jesus atoned for people's sins, they believe that everyone can now go to heaven, even sinners. But some Christians, such as some Calvinists, believe that it says in the Bible that Jesus died to save only people who believe in him, sometimes called the 'elect'. This would suggest that non-Christians cannot go to heaven, no matter how well they live their lives.

Verdict – needs developing

• A question that asks you to *evaluate* something is asking you to consider different viewpoints, including your own, in relation to a particular issue. You must refer to Christianity, fully evaluate the statement and provide a reasoned judgement in the form of a conclusion in order to gain the highest marks.

• This answer uses accurate knowledge and understanding of Christian beliefs about life after death to develop simple arguments.

• It considers more than one Christian point of view.

• However, it does not discuss enough of the issues raised by the question for it to be considered a good answer.

• The spelling, punctuation and grammar are accurate, but very few specialist terms have been used.

• It also fails to make connections between all the elements in the question. For example, it does not explain the connection between the Bible and Calvinist beliefs.

• No attempt is made to draw a justified conclusion.

Christianity Paper 1, part d)

d) 'Jesus died so that everyone can go to heaven.'
Evaluate this statement, considering arguments for and against.

(15 marks)

Sample answer 2

Christians believe that Jesus died to bring salvation to a sinful world. This is known as the atonement. It is rooted in the Christian belief in God's omnibenevolence. An all-loving God would surely not want anyone to suffer in hell. In support of this belief they can quote the teaching of St Paul to the Romans, who says that because God loves us 'He gave His own Son for us all'. Because Jesus atoned for people's sins they believe that everyone who repents can now go to heaven, even the greatest sinners. For some Christians, that also means that those who do not believe in Christ can go to heaven, provided they have tried to live a good life and are sorry for their bad deeds.

However, some Christians, such as Calvinists, have a theological belief known as pre-destination. This means that only some people have been chosen by God for salvation. John Calvin said explicitly in his 'Institutes' that some are destined for eternal life and some for eternal death. As a consequence of this belief, they say that Jesus died to save only people who believe in him; these people are sometimes called the 'elect'. To support his belief they could quote from the words of St John's Gospel, where Jesus said, 'whoever refuses to believe is dead already'. This would mean that non-believers, and even some Christians, cannot get into heaven.

This is a difficult problem to resolve. Both sides of the discussion can quote directly from the Bible to support their views. However, it seems difficult to reconcile the Christian belief in God as all-loving with a rejection of a very large part of the people he created. This is because the belief in an all-loving God is fundamental to most theists, alongside belief in God as omnipotent. The belief in God as a just judge does suggest that those who do not repent of their bad deeds need to be punished. But human beings are not perfect. Someone who is sorry for bad deeds could be a good human being. Therefore I would have to conclude that the Christian God would accept all such good people into heaven.

Verdict – strong

- This answer demonstrates an accurate understanding of Christian beliefs.
- There are two different responses, one from another Christian tradition.
- In both responses there is evidence of a logical chain of reasoning, which makes connections between all the elements in the question.
- A clear and well-argued attempt is made to draw a justified conclusion based on the arguments.
- The spelling, punctuation and grammar are accurate, and there is evidence of the appropriate use of specialist terms, such as 'pre-destination' and 'omnibenevolence'.

Glossary

abortion deliberate termination of pregnancy by removal and destruction of the foetus

Abbot the head of a monastery

absolution the act of forgiving someone for their sins

active euthanasia the ending of a person's life by direct intervention, such as administering a lethal dose of drugs

advocate for women's rights the belief that women should have the same rights and opportunities as men

agape a selfless and unconditional type of love

agnostic someone who believes there is no proof a god exists

amoral to lack a moral sense or awareness of right or wrong

Anglicans members of the Church of England

annulment a marriage terminated by the Church because it was not valid

anthropogeny the study of human origins

Apostles' Creed an early statement of Christian belief

Ash Wednesday the first day of Lent. In some Churches, penitents receive the sign of the Cross in ashes on their forehead

assisted dying when someone who is terminally ill is helped to die usually by a doctor prescribing lethal drugs

atheist someone who does not believe in the existence of a god

atonement reconciliation between God and humanity through Jesus' sacrifice on the cross

Big Bang theory the theory that an enormous explosion started the universe around 15 billion years ago

bioethics the study of what is right and wrong in biological and medical research

blasphemy to cause offence in referring to religious figures or religious ideas

catechism a summary of the principles of Christian belief in the form of questions and answers. However, the catechism of the Catholic Church is not written in this format and is, instead, a summary of the official teachings of Catholic beliefs

celibate abstaining from marriage and sexual relationships

Ceremony of Dedication a ceremony in which parents thank God for the birth of their child and make promises about how they will look after their baby

chants a repetitive song or verse, usually part of a religious ritual

charismatic faith groups groups of Christians that emphasise the work of the Holy Spirit, spiritual gifts and modern-day miracles

civil marriage a legal marriage that is conducted without a religious ceremony

civil partnership a legal union between two people of the same sex

colonisation to establish control over the indigenous people of another country

cohabitation two people who live together in an emotional and/or sexual relationship without being married

colonisation to establish a community or settlement in a new area

commit adultery a married person having a sexual relationship with someone to whom they are not married

commodity a raw material or product that can be traded, bought or sold

confirmation a ceremony held when a child is old enough to confirm the promises made on their behalf at the baptism

confirmed a person who has a firmly established belief or way or life

covenant a formal agreement or contract

congregation a group of people who have come together for worship and prayer

consecrated something declared holy, usually the Christian belief that bread and wine represent the body and blood of Jesus Christ

cosmologists scientists who investigate the development of the Universe. Modern cosmology is dominated by the Big Bang theory

Creationism the belief that the creation of the universe happened in exactly the way Genesis describes it

creationists a name given to Christians who interpret the bible literally and accept every word of the Genesis creation story as true

devotion religious worship

dioceses a district that is under the care of a bishop in the Christian Church

divine to be God or God-like

Divine Liturgy the primary Eucharist worship service of the Church

disciple a close follower of Jesus Christ, one of the twelve apostles

discrimination to treat someone differently because of their class, category or group rather than their individual merit

Doctrine of Double Effect when something morally good has an unwanted side effect which is morally bad

Doctrine of the Incarnation the belief that Jesus is the Son of God who came to Earth in human form

Doctrine of the Trinity the belief that God is three in one: the Father, the Son and the Holy Spirit

Doctrine of original sin the doctrine of humanity's state of sin as a result of Adam and Eve's rebellion in Eden

Easter the Christian festival to commemorate the resurrection of Jesus Christ

Easter Sunday the day when Easter is celebrated

ecumenical different Christian denominations working together

ecumenism the aim to promote unity among the world's Christian Churches

egalitarian the belief that all people are equal and should be granted the same rights and opportunities

electoral register an official list of people who are entitled to vote in an election

encyclical a paper letter that is sent to all the Bishops of the Roman Catholic Church

end times the time leading up to Judgement Day

ensoulment the moment at which a human being receives a soul

evangelise attempt to persuade someone to convert to Christianity

evil actions done by humans that are immoral and cause suffering

environmentalism concern with protecting the natural environment

eros sexual love and desire, named after the Greek god of love

eschatology the study of religion in relation to death, judgement and the end of the world

euthanasia intentionally killing someone for their benefit

Eucharist the Christian ceremony commemorating the Last Supper, in which bread and wine are consecrated and consumed

extreme unction anointing the sick, one of the seven Catholic sacraments

extrinsic something that is not part of the essential characteristic of a person or thing

the fall the disobedience of Adam and Eve resulting in their expulsion from Eden

festival a special occasion in the Church when an important event is celebrated

general revelations belief that knowledge of God can be discovered through natural means, such as observations of nature and the universe

glossolalia speaking in an unknown language, or tongues, during religious worship

Good Friday the Friday in Holy week, commemorating the day when Christ was executed

gospels one of the four books of the New Testament that relate the stories of Jesus Christ in his life on earth

grace virtue and kindness that is freely given to all humans by God

green Christianity Christian views on nature and the environment

hangings the practice of killing someone by dropping them with a rope tied around their neck, usually a form of capital punishment

heaven the place, or state, in which souls will be united with God after death

hell a place that some Christians believe is a punishment after death for those souls that are not free from sin; it is often referred to as a place of torment or suffering without God

holy a religious or pure person or thing

Holy Communion the Christian ceremony commemorating the Last Supper, in which bread and wine are consecrated and consumed

Holy Matrimony a phrase used by Christians to describe marriage

Holy Saturday the Saturday before Easter Sunday

Holy Week the week before Easter, when Christians recall the last week of Christ's life on Earth

homosexuality to be attracted to someone of the same sex

hospice care a place that looks after the wellbeing of those with terminal and life-limiting illnesses

humanism a belief that people's spiritual and emotional needs can be satisfied without following a religion

Humanae Vitae an encyclical (letter), written by Pope Paul VI in 1986, discussing married love, responsible parenthood and contraception

Hypostatic Union the combination of God and human natures in Jesus Christ

icons a devotional painting of Jesus Christ or other holy figure

incarnation the doctrine that God took human form in Jesus Christ

integrity an honest person with strong moral principles

immoral to behave in a way that does not conform to accepted standards of morality

immortal and everlasting an immortal being, such as God, or a soul that will live forever

interfaith activities such as marriage and religious services involving members of different religions

intrinsic being an important and essential characteristic of a person or thing

Irenaean theodicy Irenaeus' defence that argues God is not responsible for creating evil and since humans have not developed into perfect beings, suffering and evil is necessary for this development

Job the central figure in the Book of Job, in the Bible, who remains faithful to God despite all his suffering

justification by faith God's act of removing the penalty of a sin while at the same time declaring a sinner righteous through Christ's sacrifice

Last Judgement the belief that humankind will be judged at the end of the world

The Last Supper the final meal Jesus shared with his disciples

lectionary passages from the bible appointed to be read at a Church service

lectern a tall stand with a sloping top used to hold books or readings, from which someone can read from while stood up

Lent the 40 days leading up to Easter

liturgical worship worship that follows a planned set of prayers and rites

living will a written document in which a person declares how they would like to be treated if they become so ill that they cannot communicate their wishes

martyr a person who suffers or is killed for their religious beliefs

Mass a name for the Eucharist

Maundy Thursday the Thursday in Holy Week, commemorating the Last Supper

minister and clergy a religious leader and member or the clergy

miracle an unusual and extraordinary event that is not explained by scientific laws and is therefore attributed to divine intervention

monastery a building in which monks live and follow religious vows

monks a group of men who live together following religious vows

monogamy being married or in a sexual relationship with one person only

monotheistic the belief that there is only one God

moral issues concerned with whether an action is right or wrong

Moral Change Theory the idea that Jesus' action set an example for human beings, which, if followed, would restore their relationship with God

nativity the birth of Jesus Christ, which is celebrated at Christmas

naturalist an expert or student of plants and animals

natural moral law the idea that there is a natural order to our world that should be followed

natural selection the process where the species that are poorly adapted to their environment do not survive and become extinct, also known as 'survival of the fittest'

natural theology knowledge of God that is based on observed facts and experience

New Testament collection of 27 books forming the second section of the Christian Bible

Nicene Creed a statement of Christian belief in the Trinity

non-liturgical worship worship that is conducted without a specific set of prayers and rites

offertory the offering of bread and wine at the Eucharist and the donation and collection of money at a Church service

Old Testament that part of the Christian Bible which the Christian Church shares with Judaism, comprising 39 books covering the Hebrew Canon, and in the case of certain denominations, some books of the Apocrypha

omnipresent to be present everywhere and all at the same time

ordained to officially make someone a priest or religious leader

ordination the action of ordaining someone in holy orders

pagan a person who holds religious beliefs that do not belong to the main religions of the world

palliative care care for the terminally ill that seeks to manage their symptoms rather than cure them of the underlying illness

parable a story used to illustrate a moral lesson or religious idea, as told by Jesus in the Gospels

parish an area cared for by one priest with its own Church

parousia a term that describes the Second Coming of Jesus Christ

The Passion (of Jesus Christ) the sufferings of Jesus Christ, especially in the time leading up to his crucifixion

passive euthanasia ending someone's life by not doing something that could prolong their life further

pastoral care emotional and spiritual support

patriarchal relating to a social organisation controlled by a male authority

Penal Substitution Theory the doctrine that Jesus Christ died to atone for our sins

penance an act that demonstrates how remorseful you feel about something you have done

Pentecost when the Holy Spirit came down upon the apostles, after the ascension of Jesus on the seventh Sunday after Easter

philia a strong liking or friendship

pilgrimage a journey undertaken for spiritual reasons, often a journey to a shrine or holy place

polygamy being legally married to more than one person at a time

prayer an attempt to communicate with God, usually through words

prefect an important figure who may enforce discipline in certain countries

prejudice an unreasonable opinion that is formed without knowledge or experience

pro-choice advocating the right for a woman to have a choice about whether or not to have an abortion

procreate to reproduce

pro-life opposed to both abortion and euthanasia

prophet a person who is believed to have a special power that enables them to communicate the will of God

proselytise to try and persuade someone to change their religion and way of life to match your own

pulpit a raised place in a Church from which the minister speaks to people during a ceremony

purgatory a place of suffering where the souls of sinners are purified before being allowed to enter heaven

quality of life the level of satisfaction and happiness experienced by an individual or group

Ransom Theory a theory of atonement that, in order to free humanity from sin, God agreed to sacrifice Jesus Christ as a ransom to be paid to the devil

receptive ecumenism being receptive to advice from other religions in order to improve one's own

redemption the idea that sins can be forgiven and a person can be redeemed

registrar an official who is responsible for maintaining official records of births, deaths and marriages

reincarnation the rebirth of a soul into another body

repent to feel sincere regret or remorse for one's actions

resurrection the belief that Jesus Christ rose from the dead after his execution

retreat to move away from a difficult situation

rites a religious ceremony

sacrament a ceremony regarded as an outward visible sign of an inward spiritual grace

sacred holy; something or somewhere with particular religious meaning

salvation being saved from harm or ruin, such as Jesus' sacrifice to save humanity from their sins

same-sex relationship to be in a sexual relationship with someone of the same sex

Sanhedrin the highest court of justice in Ancient Jerusalem

secular having a view of the world which is not religious

sermon a talk given by a minister which highlights an important topic or issue

sexism/sexist to discriminate against a sex on the basis that one sex is superior to the other

shrine a place that is regarded as holy because of its association with a holy person or event

situation ethics the doctrine of flexibility in applying moral laws depending on the situation

storge love of community and family

soul a non-physical and immortal part of the body that continues after death and is the connection with God

special revelations belief that knowledge of God can be discovered through supernatural means, such as miracles or the scriptures

stereotype a widely held belief and image about a particular type of person or thing

stewardship the God-given right or responsibility to care for and manage the world

theist someone who believes in the existence of God or a creator of the universe

theological the study of religion

theory of evolution the gradual development of species over millions of years

theory of the expanding universe the belief that, after the Big Bang, the universe continues to expand

tithing the Christian practice of giving one-tenth of their income to charity

transcendent beyond the level of physical human experience

transmigration the passing of a soul into a different body after death

universe all existing physical matter, such as stars and planets and space

values principles or standards of behaviour

veneration to honour or worship a person or thing

vestments the clothes worn by the clergy or choristers during Church services

voluntary euthanasia the situation where someone dying in pain asks a doctor to end their life painlessly

worship pay respect or tribute to someone or something

Acknowledgements

Acknowledgements

The author and publisher would like to thank the following individuals and organisations for permission to reproduce photographs:

(Key: b-bottom; c-centre; l-left; r-right; t-top)

Alamy Images: Adrian Buck 105, Ashley Cooper 71, Christopher Scott 133b, 133b, Danny Callcut 70b, FineArt 17, GL Archive 109, Hemis 52, imageBROKER 125, Ivy Close Images 95, Liszt collection 25, Mark Boulton 133t, Melvyn Longhurst 132/2, North Wind Picture Archives 117, robertharding 44, Werner Otto 19; **Bridgeman Art Library Ltd:** Christ Pantocrator (encaustic on panel), Byzantine School, (6th century) / Monastery of Saint Catherine, Mount Sinai, Egypt / Photo © Zev Radovan 15l, Earthly Paradise (panel), Brueghel, Jan the Younger (1601-78) / Galerie de Jonckheere, Paris, France 12, Garden of Eden (oil on canvas), Savery, Roelandt Jacobsz. (1576-1639) / Faringdon Collection, Buscot, Oxon, UK 6; **Fotolia. com:** gaborphotos 74, razyph 72-73, Syda Productions 36-37; **Getty Images:** ALBERTO PIZZOLI 97b, db2stock 85, DEA / A. DAGLI ORTI / Contributor 28, George Tsafos 40, Justin Ouellette 106 Matt Cardy / Stringer 60, Merten Snijders 54, Oleh Slobodeniuk 78, Paul Bradbury 48, Rischgitz / Stringer 64, YOMIURI SHIMBUN / Stringer 27; **London School of Economics Library:** 97t; NASA: JPL-Caltech / ESA / Harvard-Smithsonian CfA 108; **Operation Noah:** 133c; **Rex Shutterstock:** Clare Kendall / REX 77; **Science Photo Library Ltd:** GABRIELLE VOINOT / LOOK AT SCIENCES 112, PASCAL BROZE / REPORTERS 130, SCIEPRO 119t, 119c, 119b, 119b; **Shutterstock. com:** Keith McIntyre 18, Renata Sedmakova 22; **Tearfund:** 99; **The Art Archive:** Kunsthistorisches Museum Vienna / Mondadori Portfolio / Electa 8; **The Salvation Army:** 70t; **www.heqiart.com:** www.heqigallery.com 124

Cover images: *Front:* Corbis: Heide Benser
Picture Research by: Caitlin Swain
All other images © Pearson Education

Text
The author and publisher are grateful to the following for permission to reproduce copyright material:
All Bible scripture quotations taken from the Holy Bible, New International Version Anglicised Copyright © 1979, 1984, 2011 Biblica. Used by permission of Hodder & Stoughton Ltd, an Hachette UK company. All rights reserved.
Page 9: Quote from 'The Nicene Creed', Catechism of the Catholic Church © Libreria Editrice Vaticana, Citta del Vaticano 1993. Page 35: Quote from 'The Apostles' Creed', Catechism of the Catholic Church © Libreria Editrice Vaticana, Citta del Vaticano (1993). Page 39: 'Liturgy and the liturgical year', https://www. churchofengland.org © The Church of England. Page 51: Quote from http://www.iona.org.uk © Iona Community. Page 58l: Quote from Baroness Wilcox of Plymouth, Chairman of London's Diocesan Advisory Committee (2014) © Parliament UK. Page 58r: Quote from the banner heading of https://www.churchofengland.org © The Church of England. Page 59: Quotes from https://www.cuf.org.uk/ how-we-help © Church Urban Fund. Page 63: Quote from http:// www.christianaid.org.uk © Christian Aid. Page 64: Quote from https://www.churchofengland.org © The Church of England. Page 69: C.S. Lewis quote from *Shadowlands* (1993) © William Nicholson. Page 70: 'A statement on baptism' taken from the Salvation Army website (2016) © Salvation Army. Page 81r: Quote from https:// www.churchofengland.org © The Church of England. Page 81b:

Quote from 'Church of England Marriage Ceremony', *Book of Common Prayer* sourced from https://www.churchofengland.org (2016) © The Church of England. Page 82: Quote from http://www. humanismforschools.org.uk © The British Humanist Association. Page 84: Quote from http://www.parishofstfaith.org.uk (2016) © Parish of St. Faith. Page 88: Quote from https://humanism. org.uk © The British Humanist Association. Page 89: Quote from *Humanae Vitae no. 14*, an encyclical letter of Pope Paul VI, issued on 25 July 1968 © Vatican Publishing House. Page 91: Quote from https://www.churchofengland.org © The Church of England. Page 92: Quote from General Synod of the Catholic Bishops (2005) © Vatican Publishing House. Page 98: Quote from 'Gender Justice for All: achieving just and equitable power relations between women and men' (July 2014), sourced from https://www.christianaid. uk © Christian Aid. Page 99: Quotes from http://www.tearfund.org © Tearfund. Page 103: Quote from 'Why get married in a church?' sourced from https://www.yourchurchwedding.org © The Church of England. Page 116: Quote from 'Special agenda IV Diocesan Synod motions compatibility of science and Christian belief', Diocese of Manchester (2009) © The Church of England. Page 119: Quote from www.nhs.uk (2016) © Health & Social Care Information Centre. Page 120t: Quote from 'Abortion: an ethical discussion. Church of England Assembly Board for Social Responsibility, Church Information Office' (1965) © The Church of England. Page 120c: Quote from 'C of E view of abortion' (1988), sourced from https:// www.churchofengland.org © The Church of England. Page 120b: Quote from 'C of E opposition to abortion', sourced from https:// www.churchofengland.org © The Church of England. Page 121: Quote from Pope John Paul II, Evangelium Vitae, 62, (1995) © Vatican Publishing House.
Page 125t: Quotes from Richard Dawkins, Guardian News, 'Richard Dawkins 'Wonders' What Happens After We Die'. (2013) © Guardian News and Media Ltd. Page 125b: Quote from http://www. humanismforschools.org.uk © The British Humanist Association. Page 129l: Quote from 'Dignity in Dying', sourced from http://www. DignityinDying.org.uk © Dignity in Dying. Page 129r: Quote from Rev Dr Brendan McCarthy, Church of England national adviser on medical ethics sourced from https://www.churchofengland.org (2015) © The Church of England. Page 130: Quote from https:// humanism.org.uk © The British Humanist Association. Page 132: Quote from the Archbishop of Canterbury, Justin Welby. Sourced from http://www.archbishopofcanterbury.org © The office of the Archbishop of Canterbury, Lambeth Palace. Page 133: Quote from 'Operation Noah - Christian response to climate change' sourced from http://operationnoah.org © Operation Noah. Page 134t: Quote from *Quaker Faith and Practice*, 42, Chapter 1 © Religious Society of Friends (Quakers). Page 134b: Quote from Andrew Linzey on vegetarianism © Andrew Linzey. Page 137: Quote from Richard Dawkins © Richard Dawkins. Page 137: Quote from Mother Teresa, sourced from 'Nobel Lectures, Peace 1971-1980', World Scientific Publishing Co., Singapore, (1997) © The Nobel Foundation. Page 138, Source 1: 'UK parliament votes heavily against assisted suicide', John McDermott and Sarah Neville, The Financial Times (2016) © The Financial Times Limited. All Rights Reserved. Page 138, Source 2: Quote regarding the Archbishop of Canterbury, Justin Welby, from The Observer (2015) © Guardian News and Media Ltd. Page 138, Source 2: Quote regarding the former Archbishop of Canterbury, George Carey, from The Telegraph (2015) © Telegraph Media Group Ltd.

All reproduced with kind permission.